KEEPING THE B...

Did You Know . . . ? when Bond started drinking Bollinger champagne in Moonraker, the firm was unable to match the sudden worldwide demand for the high-class tipple.

Did You Know . . . ? stuntman Bob Simmons, associated with the series throughout the last twenty-five years, was originally in the running for the role of 007.

Did You Know . . . ? the scale model of the Goldfinger Aston Martin made by Corgi in the 1960s sold more than seven million and is still available today.

Did You Know . . . ? Bond is responsible for the death of more than 120 characters during the series.

Did you know? Read on for more amazing facts...

Keeping The British End Up

Roger Ryan and
Martin Sterling

CORONET BOOKS
Hodder and Stoughton

British Library C.I.P.

Keeping the British end up.
    1. James Bond films   2. Fleming, Ian,
    1908–1964—Characters—James Bond
    3. Bond, James (fictitious character)
    I. Title   II. Sterling, Martin
    791.43'52   PN1995.9.J3

ISBN 0 340 41429 4

Printed and bound in Great Britain
for Hodder and Stoughton
Paperbacks, a division of Hodder and
Stoughton Ltd., Mill Road,
Dunton Green, Sevenoaks, Kent
TN13 2YA.
(Editorial Office: 47 Bedford Square,
London WC1B 3DP) by
Cox & Wyman Ltd., Reading

ACKNOWLEDGEMENTS

We would like to thank Albert R. Broccoli, Michael G. Wilson and all at Eon Productions, Derek Coyte, Charles Juroe, Reginald Barkshire, John Parkinson of Glidrose Publications, Peter Straus of Coronet, Sue Ryan, Dorothy Twist, Lotus Cars and Aston Martin.

For his tireless support, special thanks must go to Andrew Lownie of John Farquharson, without whom this would not have been possible.

We dedicate this book to the memory of Ian Lancaster Fleming (1908–1964), creator of James Bond, and to Albert R. Broccoli for twenty-five years of screen excellence.

FOREWORD

James Bond celebrates his big screen silver jubilee in 1987. Twenty-five years' continuous production of a film series is an unparalleled feat in the film industry. No other box office character has scaled such heights of success and stayed at the top despite numerous changes in cast and crew.

Keeping The British End Up is unashamedly a book of 007 film trivia. A silver jubilee is very much a time of celebration and this is precisely the spirit we have endeavoured to capture. The book is also a tribute to Albert Broccoli and Eon Productions – the team behind the scenes. We have looked at the series from the fans' viewpoint. Rather than a pedestrian film-by-film approach we have adopted a more stylised, often tongue-in-cheek method.

Like the films, fact and fiction blend together in *Keeping The British End Up* to create an entertaining mix. The Bond series has given us much pleasure over the past twenty-five years and this we hope to share with you.

The advent of Timothy Dalton as the fourth 007, coinciding with the silver jubilee, gives an opportunity not only to look back but also view the future. The passing of time has merely underlined the fact that the appeal remains undiminished. If anything, judging by the media response to *The Living Daylights*, the success of the latest addition to the stable seems assured.

ROGER RYAN
MARTIN STERLING
MAY 1987

DR NO

CAST: JAMES BOND – Sean Connery; HONEY – Ursula Andress; DR NO – Joseph Wiseman; FELIX LEITER – Jack Lord; 'M' – Bernard Lee; MISS MONEYPENNY – Lois Maxwell; MAJOR BOOTHROYD – Peter Burton; DENT – Anthony Dawson; QUARREL – John Kitzmiller; MISS TARO – Zena Marshall; SYLVIA – Eunice Gayson; PUSS-FELLER – Lester Prendergast; STRANGWAYS – Tim Moxon; PLEYDELL-SMITH – Louis Blaazer.

Made by Eon Productions. 105 minutes. Colour. Released 1962. PRODUCERS – Albert R. Broccoli and Harry Saltzman; DIRECTOR – Terence Young; SCREENPLAY – Richard Maibaum, Joanna Harwood and Berkely Mather; MUSIC – Monty Norman; PRODUCTION DESIGNER – Ken Adam; DIRECTOR OF PHOTOGRAPHY – Ted Moore; MAIN TITLE DESIGNER – Maurice Binder; EDITOR – Peter Hunt; SPECIAL EFFECTS – Frank George.

FROM RUSSIA WITH LOVE

CAST: JAMES BOND – Sean Connery; TATIANA ROMANOVA – Daniela Bianchi; KERIM BEY – Pedro Armendariz; ROSA KLEBB – Lotte Lenya; GRANT – Robert Shaw; 'M' – Bernard Lee; MISS MONEYPENNY – Lois Maxwell; MAJOR BOOTHROYD – Desmond Llewelyn; SYLVIA – Eunice Gayson; MORZENY – Walter Gotell; VAVRA – Francis de Wolff; TRAIN CONDUCTOR – George Pastell; KERIM'S GIRL – Nadja Regin; VIDA – Aliza Gur; ZORA – Martine Beswick; KRONSTEEN – Vladek Sheybal; BELLY DANCER – Leila.

Made by Eon Productions. 116 minutes. Colour. Released 1963. PRODUCERS – Albert R. Broccoli and Harry Saltzman; DIRECTOR – Terence Young; SCREENPLAY – Richard Maibaum and Joanna Harwood; MUSIC – John Barry; TITLE SONG PERFORMED BY – Matt Monro; TITLE SONG WRITTEN BY – Lionel Bart; PRODUCTION DESIGNER – Syd Cain; DIRECTOR OF PHOTOGRAPHY – Ted Moore; MAIN TITLE DESIGNS – Robert Brownjohn and Trevor Bond; EDITOR – Peter Hunt; SPECIAL EFFECTS – John Stears and Frank George; STUNT ARRANGERS – Peter Perkins and Bob Simmons.

GOLDFINGER

CAST: JAMES BOND – Sean Connery; PUSSY GALORE – Honor Blackman; AURIC GOLDFINGER – Gert Frobe; JILL MASTERSON – Shirley Eaton; TILLY MASTERSON – Tania Mallet; ODDJOB – Harold Sakata; 'M' – Bernard Lee; 'Q' – Desmond Llewelyn; MISS MONEYPENNY – Lois Maxwell; SOLO – Martin Benson; LEITER – Cec Linder; MIDNIGHT – Bill Nagy; CAPUNGO – Alf Joint; BONITA – Nadja Regin; SMITHERS – Richard Vernon; KISCH – Michael Mellinger.

Made by Eon Productions. 109 minutes. Colour. Released 1964. PRODUCERS – Albert R. Broccoli and Harry Saltzman; DIRECTOR – Guy Hamilton; SCREEN-PLAY – Richard Maibaum and Paul Dehn; MUSIC – John Barry; TITLE SONG PERFORMED BY – Shirley Bassey; LYRICS – Leslie Bricusse and Anthony Newly; PRO-DUCTION DESIGNER – Ken Adam; DIRECTOR OF PHOTO-GRAPHY – Ted Moore; MAIN TITLE DESIGNER – Robert Brownjohn; EDITOR – Peter Hunt; SPECIAL EFFECTS – John Stears (assisted by Frank George); STUNT ARRANGER – Bob Simmons.

THUNDERBALL

CAST: JAMES BOND – Sean Connery; DOMINO DERVAL – Claudine Auger; LARGO – Adolfo Celi; FIONA – Luciana Paluzzi; LEITER – Rik Van Nutter; 'M' – Bernard Lee; 'Q' – Desmond Llewelyn; MISS MONEYPENNY – Lois Maxwell; PAULA – Martine Beswick; LIPPE – Guy Doleman; PATRICIA – Molly Peters; FOREIGN SECRETARY – Roland Culver; PINDER – Earl Cameron; DERVAL/ANGELO – Paul Stassino; MADAME BOIVARD – Rose Alba; VARGAS – Phillip Locke; GROUP CAPTAIN PRITCHARD – Leonard Sachs.

Made by Eon Productions. 130 minutes. Colour. Released 1965. PRODUCER – Kevin McClory; EXECUTIVE PRODUCERS – Albert R. Broccoli and Harry Saltzman; DIRECTOR – Terence Young; SCREENPLAY – Richard Maibaum and John Hopkins; MUSIC – John Barry; TITLE SONG PERFORMED BY – Tom Jones; LYRICS – Don Black; PRODUCTION DESIGNER – Ken Adam; DIRECTOR OF PHOTOGRAPHY – Ted Moore; MAIN TITLE DESIGNER – Maurice Binder; EDITOR – Peter Hunt; SPECIAL EFFECTS – John Stears; STUNT ARRANGER – Bob Simmons.

YOU ONLY LIVE TWICE

CAST: JAMES BOND – Sean Connery; AKI – Akiko Wakabayashi; TIGER TANAKA – Tetsuro Tamba; KISSY SUZUKI – Mie Hama; MR OSATO – Teru Shimada; HELGA – Karin Dor; ERNST STAVRO BLOFELD – Donald Pleasence; 'M' – Bernard Lee; 'Q' – Desmond Llewelyn; MISS MONEY-PENNY – Lois Maxwell; HENDERSON – Charles Gray; CHINESE GIRL – Tsai Chin.

Made by Eon Productions. 116 minutes. Colour. Released 1967. PRODUCERS – Albert R. Broccoli and Harry Saltzman; DIRECTOR – Lewis Gilbert; SCREENPLAY – Roald Dahl; MUSIC – John Barry; TITLE SONG PER-FORMED BY – Nancy Sinatra; LYRICS – Leslie Bricusse; PRODUCTION DESIGNER – Ken Adam; DIRECTOR OF PHOTOGRAPHY – Freddie Young; MAIN TITLE DESIGNER –. Maurice Binder; EDITOR – Thelma Connell; SPECIAL EFFECTS – John Stears; STUNT ARRANGER – Bob Simmons.

ON HER MAJESTY'S SECRET SERVICE

CAST: JAMES BOND – George Lazenby; TRACY – Diana Rigg; ERNST STAVRO BLOFELD – Telly Savalas; IRMA BUNT – Ilse Steppat; DRACO – Gabriele Ferzetti; CAMPBELL – Bernard Horsfall; SIR HILARY BRAY – George Baker; 'M' – Bernard Lee; MISS MONEYPENNY – Lois Maxwell; RUBY – Angela Scoular; NANCY – Catherina von Schell; ENGLISH GIRL – Joanna Lumley.

Made by Eon Productions. 140 minutes. Colour. Released 1969. PRODUCERS – Albert R. Broccoli and Harry Saltzman; DIRECTOR – Peter Hunt; SCREENPLAY – Richard Maibaum (additional dialogue by Simon Raven); MUSIC – John Barry; SONG – 'We Have All The Time In The World'; PERFORMED BY – Louis Armstrong; LYRICS – Hal David; PRODUCTION DESIGNER – Syd Cain; DIRECTOR OF PHOTOGRAPHY – Michael Reed; MAIN TITLE DESIGNER – Maurice Binder; EDITOR – John Glen; SPECIAL EFFECTS – John Stears; STUNT ARRANGER – George Leech.

DIAMONDS ARE FOREVER

CAST: JAMES BOND – Sean Connery; TIFFANY CASE – Jill St John; ERNST STAVRO BLOFELD – Charles Gray; PLENTY O'TOOLE – Lana Wood; WILLARD WHYTE – Jimmy Dean; SAXBY – Bruce Cabot; MR KIDD – Putter Smith; MR WINT – Bruce Glover; FELIX LEITER – Norman Burton; DR METZ – Joseph Furst; MORTON SLUMBER – David Bauer; 'M' – Bernard Lee; 'Q' – Desmond Llewelyn; MISS MONEYPENNY – Lois Maxwell; SHADY TREE – Leonard Barr.

Made by Eon Productions. 120 minutes. Colour. Released 1971. PRODUCERS – Albert R. Broccoli and Harry Saltzman; DIRECTOR – Guy Hamilton; SCREENPLAY – Richard Maibaum and Tom Mankiwicz; MUSIC – John Barry; TITLE SONG PERFORMED BY – Shirley Bassey; LYRICS – Don Black; PRODUCTION DESIGNER – Ken Adam; DIRECTOR OF PHOTOGRAPHY – Ted Moore; MAIN TITLE DESIGNER – Maurice Binder; EDITORS – Bert Bates and John Holmes; SPECIAL EFFECTS – Leslie Hillman and Whitey McMahan; STUNT ARRANGERS – Bob Simmons and Paul Baxley.

LIVE AND LET DIE

CAST: JAMES BOND – Roger Moore; MR BIG/KANANGA – Yaphet Kotto; SOLITAIRE – Jane Seymour; TEE HEE – Julius W. Harris; SHERIFF PEPPER – Clifton James; BARON SAMEDI – Geoffrey Holder; FELIX LEITER – David Hedison; ROSIE CARVER – Gloria Hendry; 'M' – Bernard Lee; MISS MONEYPENNY – Lois Maxwell; ADAM – Tommy Lane; WHISPER – Earl Jolly Brown; QUARREL – Roy Stewart; STRUTTER – Lon Satton; MRS BELL – Ruth Kempf; CHARLIE – Joie Chitwood; BEAUTIFUL GIRL – Madeline Smith; SINGER – B. J. Arnau.

Made by Eon Productions. 121 minutes. Colour. Released 1973. PRODUCERS – Albert R. Broccoli and Harry Saltzman; DIRECTOR – Guy Hamilton; SCREEN-PLAY – Tom Mankiewicz; MUSIC – George Martin; TITLE SONG COMPOSED BY – Paul and Linda McCartney; TITLE SONG PERFORMED BY – Paul McCartney and Wings; PRODUCTION DESIGNER – Syd Cain; DIRECTOR OF PHOTO-GRAPHY – Bob Kindred; MAIN TITLE DESIGNER – Maurice Binder; EDITORS – John Shirley and Raymond Poulton; SPECIAL EFFECTS – Derek Meddings; STUNT CO-ORDINATORS – Ross Kananga, Joie Chitwood, Jerry Comeaux and Bob Simmons.

THE MAN WITH THE GOLDEN GUN

CAST: JAMES BOND – Roger Moore; SCARAMANGA – Christopher Lee; MARY GOODNIGHT – Britt Ekland; ANDREA ANDERS – Maud Adams; NICK NACK – Herve Villechaize; 'M' – Bernard Lee; 'Q' – Desmond Llewelyn; MISS MONEYPENNY – Lois Maxwell; COLTHORPE – James Cossins; HI FAT – Richard Loo; J. W. PEPPER – Clifton James; HIP – Soon-Taik-Oh.

Made by Eon Productions. 125 minutes. Colour. Released 1974. PRODUCERS – Albert R. Broccoli and Harry Saltzman; DIRECTOR – Guy Hamilton; SCREENPLAY – Richard Maibaum and Tom Mankiewcz; MUSIC – John Barry; TITLE SONG PERFORMED BY – Lulu; LYRICS – Don Black; PRODUCTION DESIGNER – Peter Murton; DIRECTOR OF PHOTOGRAPHY – Ted Moore and Oswald Morris; MAIN TITLE DESIGNER – Maurice Binder; EDITORS – John Shirley and Raymond Poulton; SPECIAL EFFECTS – John Stears; STUNT CO-ORDINATOR – W. J. Milligan Jr.

THE SPY WHO LOVED ME

CAST: JAMES BOND – Roger Moore; MAJOR ANYA AMASOVA – Barbara Bach; STROMBERG – Curt Jurgens; JAWS – Richard Kiel; NAOMI – Caroline Munro; 'M' – Bernard Lee; 'Q' – Desmond Llewelyn; MISS MONEYPENNY – Lois Maxwell; GOGOL – Walter Gotell; MINISTER OF DEFENCE – Geoffrey Keen; CAPTAIN CARTER – Shane Rimmer; COMMANDER TALBOT – Bryan Marshall; SERGEI – Michael Billington; FELICCA – Olga Bisera; SHEIK HOSSEIN – Edward de Souza; MAX KALBA – Vernon Dobcheff.

Made by Eon Productions. 125 minutes. Colour. Released 1977. PRODUCER – Albert R. Broccoli; DIRECTOR – Lewis Gilbert; SCREENPLAY – Richard Maibaum and Christopher Wood; MUSIC – Marvin Hamlisch; TITLE SONG PERFORMED BY – Carly Simon; LYRICS – Carole Bayer Sager; PRODUCTION DESIGNER – Ken Adam; DIRECTOR OF PHOTOGRAPHY – Claude Renoir; MAIN TITLE DESIGNER – Maurice Binder; EDITOR – John Glen; SPECIAL EFFECTS SUPERVISOR – Derek Meddings; ACTION SEQUENCES ARRANGER – Bob Simmons.

MOONRAKER

CAST: JAMES BOND: – Roger Moore; HOLLY GOODHEAD – Lois Chiles; HUGO DRAX – Michael Lonsdale; JAWS – Richard Kiel; CORRINNE DUFOUR – Corrinne Clery; CHANG – Toshiro Suga; 'M' – Bernard Lee; 'Q' – Desmond Llewelyn; MISS MONEYPENNY – Lois Maxwell; MINISTER OF DEFENCE – Geoffrey Keen; GOGOL – Walter Gotell; DOLLY – Blanche Ravalec; MANUELA – Emily Boulton; CONSUMPTIVE ITALIAN – Alfie Bass.

Made by Eon Productions (London) and Les Productions Artistes Associés (Paris). 126 minutes. Colour. Released 1979. PRODUCER – Albert R. Broccoli; DIRECTOR – Lewis Gilbert; SCREENPLAY – Christopher Wood; MUSIC – John Barry; TITLE SONG PERFORMED BY – Shirley Bassey; LYRICS – Hal David; PRODUCTION DESIGNER – Ken Adam; DIRECTOR OF PHOTOGRAPHY – Jean Tournier; MAIN TITLE DESIGNER – Maurice Binder; EDITOR – John Glen; SPECIAL EFFECTS SUPERVISOR – Derek Meddings; ACTION SEQUENCES ARRANGER – Bob Simmons.

FOR YOUR EYES ONLY

CAST: JAMES BOND – Roger Moore; MELINA – Carole Bouquet; COLUMBO – Topol; BIBI – Lynn-Holly Johnson; KRISTATOS – Julian Glover; LISL – Cassandra Harris; BRINK – Jill Bennett; LOCQUE – Michael Gothard; KRIEGLER – John Wyman; HAVELOCK – Jack Hedley; MISS MONEYPENNY – Lois Maxwell; 'Q' – Desmond Llewelyn; MINISTER OF DEFENCE – Geoffrey Keen; GOGOL – Walter Gotell; TANNER – James Villiers; FERRARA – John Moreno; CLAUS – Charles Dance.

Made by Eon Productions. 127 minutes. Colour. Released 1981. PRODUCER – Albert R. Broccoli; DIRECTOR – John Glen; SCREENPLAY – Richard Maibaum and Michael G. Wilson; MUSIC – Bill Conti; TITLE SONG PERFORMED BY – Sheena Easton; LYRICS – Michael Leeson; PRODUCTION DESIGNER – Peter Lamont; DIRECTOR OF PHOTOGRAPHY – Alan Hume; MAIN TITLE DESIGNER – Maurice Binder; EDITOR – John Grover; SPECIAL EFFECTS SUPERVISOR – Derek Meddings; ACTION SEQUENCES ARRANGER – Bob Simmons.

OCTOPUSSY

CAST: JAMES BOND – Roger Moore; OCTOPUSSY – Maud Adams; KAMAL KHAN – Louis Jourdan; MAGDA – Kristina Wayborn; GOBINA – Kabir Bedi; ORLOV – Steven Berkoff; TWIN ONE – David Meyer; TWIN TWO – Tony Meyer; VIJAY – Vijay Amritraj; 'Q' – Desmond Llewelyn; 'M' – Robert Brown; MISS MONEYPENNY – Lois Maxwell; PENELOPE SMALLBONE – Michaela Clavell; GOGOL – Walter Gotell; MINISTER OF DEFENCE – Geoffrey Keen; 009 – Andy Bradford.

Made by Eon Productions. 130 minutes. Colour. Released 1983. PRODUCER – Albert R. Broccoli; DIRECTOR – John Glen; SCREEN STORY AND SCREENPLAY – George McDonald, Fraser and Richard Maibaum and Michael G. Wilson; MUSIC – John Barry; LYRICS – Tim Rice; TITLE SONG PERFORMED BY – Rita Coolidge; PRODUCTION DESIGNER – Peter Lamont; DIRECTOR OF PHOTOGRAPHY – Alan Hume; MAIN TITLE DESIGNER – Maurice Binder; EDITORS – Peter Davies and Henry Richardson; SPECIAL EFFECTS SUPERVISOR – John Richardson; ACTION SEQUENCES ARRANGER – Bob Simmons.

A VIEW TO A KILL

CAST: JAMES BOND – Roger Moore; MAX ZORIN – Christopher Walken; STACEY SUTTON – Tanya Roberts; MAY DAY – Grace Jones; TIBBETT – Patrick MacNee; SCARPINE – Patrick Bauchau; CHUCK LEE – David Yip; POLA IVANOVA – Fiona Fullerton; BOB CONLEY – Manning Redwood; JENNY FLEX – Alison Doody; DR CARL MORTNER – Willoughby Gray; 'Q' – Desmond Llewelyn; 'M' – Robert Brown; MISS MONEYPENNY – Lois Maxwell; GENERAL GOGOL – Walter Gotell; MINISTER OF DEFENCE – Geoffrey Keen; KIMBERLEY JONES – Mary Stavin.

Made by Eon Productions. 126 minutes. Colour. Released 1985. PRODUCERS – Albert R. Broccoli and Michael G. Wilson; DIRECTOR – John Glen; SCREENPLAY – Richard Maibaum and Michael G. Wilson; MUSIC – John Barry; TITLE SONG – Duran Duran; TITLE SONG COMPOSED BY – Duran Duran and John Barry; PRODUCTION DESIGNER – Peter Lamont; DIRECTOR OF PHOTOGRAPHY – Alan Hume; MAIN TITLE DESIGNER – Maurice Binder; EDITOR – Peter Davies; SPECIAL EFFECTS SUPERVISOR – John Richardson; ACTION SEQUENCES ARRANGER – Martin Grace.

QUOTE, UNQUOTE

'I don't like guns. I don't like what they do to people nor the violence they represent.' *Roger Moore, 1981*

'The critics don't seem to be fond of us... but we'll manage as long as we keep going to the bank.' *Cubby Broccoli, 1985*

'I'd like to kill that damned James Bond.' *Sean Connery, 1966*

'When sketching out a Bond film... we try to think of all the basic things that thrill people, that really make them frightened.' *John Glen, 1981*

'I don't believe in that sort of hero. Heroes to me are policeman and fireman.' *Roger Moore on Bond, 1981*

'Bond films are so outrageous... There is no such thing as a spy who can walk anywhere in the world and every bartender recognises him and says, "Ah, Mr Bond. A vodka martini, shaken not stirred." Spies aren't like that.' *Roger Moore, 1985*

'I will cheerfully play the old-fashioned male chauvinist for the camera, but off screen I wouldn't dare.' *Timothy Dalton, 1986*

'Those who've read the book are likely to be disappointed, but those who haven't will find it a wonderful movie.' *Ian Fleming, writing on the release of Dr No, 1962*

'It is like the prefect taking over from the school bully.'
Film critic Alexander Walker commenting on Roger Moore's début as Bond in 1973

'The Bond films came at just the right time. Kitchen-sink realistic pictures were over, and we gave them a new mythology.' *Harry Saltzman, 1966*

'You don't see Bond kill just for the sake of it . . . he always kills in self-defence or for a good reason – for entertainment, or to progress the plot.' *Cubby Broccoli, 1966*

'I've only read one of the Bond books. They lack humour, that's their trouble.' *Sean Connery, 1966*

DID YOU KNOW?

... when Bond started drinking Bollinger champagne in Moonraker, the firm was unable to match the sudden worldwide demand for the high-class tipple.

... stuntman Bob Simmons, associated with the series throughout the last twenty-five years, was originally in the running for the role of 007.

... Roger Moore and Lois Maxwell were in the same class at the Royal Academy of Dramatic Art in London during the 1940s. Miss Maxwell was then known by her real name, Lois Hooker. Little were they to know that they would share scenes as Bond and Miss Moneypenny in seven Bond films between 1973 and 1985.

... Cary Grant and James Mason both agreed in principle to play Bond in *Dr No*. But because Grant would only commit himself for one picture and Mason just two, both were turned down in favour of Sean Connery. A willingness to sign a multi-picture contract was one of the factors that won Connery the role.

... shooting on the first Bond adventure, *Dr No*, took place in Jamaica on January 16, 1962. The first day's filming at Pinewood Studios, the series home for a quarter of a century, took place on Monday, February 26, 1962.

... when Bond asked for a vodka, consumption in Britain

alone rose by 10,000 gallons a year, bringing a smile, perhaps, to the faces of 007's erstwhile critics in the Soviet Union.

... the scale model of the Goldfinger Aston Martin made by Corgi in the 1960s sold more than seven million and is still available today.

... the helicopter dog fight above Blofeld's (Donald Pleasence) Japanese volcano base in *You Only Live Twice* was filmed in Spain over Torremolinos on the Costa del Sol. And the motor boat chase climax in *From Russia With Love* set near Venice was shot on the west coast of Scotland.

... Sean Connery wore a toupée in his later films in the series. But for Sean it was a case of hair today, gone tomorrow, as he always discarded the wig off set.

... according to sources close to the production company, the champagne in the series was always ginger ale and not in the slightest bit alcoholic. The whisky, in turn, was watered down coffee and the Martinis were neither stirred nor shaken but pure water.

... Cubby Broccoli was awarded in 1982 the highest honour the film industry can bestow on a producer. The Academy of Motion Pictures Arts and Sciences presented him with the Irving G. Thalberg Award for 'continued production excellence'. This gave Broccoli a place in the cinematic hall of fame. He joined such giants as David O. Selznick, Alfred Hitchcock, Walt Disney and Cecil B. De Mille who have also been presented with the honour.

... Two of the most daring stunts performed in the series, the pre-credits ski jump-cum-parachute decent in *The Sphy Who Loved Me*, and the one hundred foot fall from the top of a monastery in Greece in *For Your Eyes Only*, were both performed by stunt man Rick Sylvester.

Sylvester was paid thirty thousand dollars for the ski jump off the 3000-foot peak on Baffin Island.

... the go-ahead from United Artists to start the first Bond film came on June 20, 1961, at a meeting in New York between Arthur Krim, president of United Artists, Cubby Broccoli and Harry Saltzman.

... there is a church in Toronto, Canada, named the St James Bond United Church.

... Jamaica has featured twice as a fictional island in the series. In *Dr No*, the Crab Key beach sequences were filmed on the north of the island, while in *Live And Let Die*, Jamaica was the setting for the island of San Monique, headquarters for Dr Kananga (Yaphet Kotto).

... so confident were Albert R. Broccoli and Harry Saltzman during the making of *Dr No* that the first film was going to be a success, that the duo promised that 007 would return in *From Russia With Love*. This became a tradition in the series that the title of the next film is announced at the end of the credits of the current feature. The only time this was not the case was at the conclusion of *A View To A Kill* which promises only that Bond will return.

... Ian Fleming's original name for the decoding device in *From Russia With Love* was the Spektor, but the film producers decided to change this to Lektor to avoid confusing the audience when the SPECTRE organisation was introduced.

... John Glen is the only director in the series to take control of four consecutive Bond films – *For Your Eyes Only*, *Octopussy*, *A View To A Kill* and *The Living Daylights*. Guy Hamilton has also directed four Bond movies. But there was a gap of seven years between the first, *Goldfinger*, and the second, *Diamonds Are Forever*.

... author Roald Dahl, the screenwriter for *You Only Live Twice*, had seen only *Goldfinger* in the series before he sat down to write his script.

... Ken Adam's volcano set for the climactic sequence of action at the conclusion of *You Only Live Twice* used more than 700 tons of structural steel, more than 200 miles of tubular steel and more than 250,000 square yards of protective canvas.

... British television journalist Alan Whicker made an hour-long documentary of the making of *You Only Live Twice* in 1967. It was the last of the Whicker shows to be made in black and white.

... the US Treasury Department refused Eon Productions permission to film inside the gold depository at Fort Knox for Goldfinger.

... despite being passed by the censor for general release in 1963, the fight between 007 and Grant (Robert Shaw) aboard the Orient Express in *From Russia With Love* is usually heavily cut in television versions throughout the world because of its supposed violent content.

... Bond features in forty-seven lovemaking scenes on screen involving thirty-eight women.

... Bond is responsible for the death of more than 120 characters during the series.

BOND FROM A-Z

ACCIDENTS: Major accidents are rare during filming due to the sheer professionalism of the crew and stuntmen who work on the series – but, inevitably, they have happened.

Celebrated cameraman John Jordan lost a foot while shooting the helicopter battle highlight of *You Only Live Twice*. A stunt helicopter was caught in an updraught and its rotors sliced through the skids of Jordan's camera helicopter and also through his foot. Jordan returned on the next film, *OHMSS*, to contribute more breathtaking aerial photography but was killed while working on another movie, *Catch-22*, in Mexico later in 1969.

Two serious accidents marred production of *For Your Eyes Only* in 1980–81. Twenty-three-year-old Italian Paola Rigon was killed during filming of the bobsleigh sequence in Cortina and a stunt girl doubling for Cassandra Harris was badly hurt when she was struck by a dune buggy during action sequences shot on the beaches of Corfu.

Martin Grace, Roger Moore's stunt double, was badly injured during the making of *Octopussy*. He was hurt when shooting one of the climactic scenes on a railway track. Fortunately, he was able to make a recovery and returned to the series as action sequence arranger on the next film, *A View To A Kill*.

ACROJET: A tiny Acrojet aircraft, with a wingspan of only twelve feet, is featured in the pre-credits sequence of *Octopussy* – a sequence that director John Glen has gone on record as saying he believes is one of the series' best. Bond is forced to fly through an aircraft hangar in his attempt to avoid a heat-seeking missile. The hangar contains a spy plane which 007 is attempting to sabotage. But the doors at the far end of the hangar are closing and blocking his escape.

Quick-thinking Bond flies through the hangar and out the other end just in time to avoid the doors closing on him. The sequence works through a clever combination of direction by Glen, editing by Peter Davies, Henry Richardson and John Grover and special effects by John Richardson. Flying the Acrojet is Corkey Fornof.

Originally, the Acrojet was to appear in *Moonraker*. A scene for the aircraft was written into one of the draft scripts.

KEN ADAM: A German Jew who once flew wartime RAF Spitfires, Adam is a true cinematic genius. His bizarre inventiveness as a production designer has been more than adequately displayed in such films as *Dr Strangelove*, *Funeral in Berlin* and *Sleuth*.

His creativeness has added much to seven Bond films: *Dr No, Goldfinger, Thunderball, You Only Live Twice, Diamonds are Forever, The Spy Who Loved Me* and *Moonraker*. His penchant for low-ceilinged rooms with sloping walls is one feature of his work that has added a great deal of atmosphere to 007 movies, while his organising abilities have made the huge sets of *Goldfinger, You Only Live Twice* and *The Spy Who Loved Me*, in particular, such a success. These three films contain the best of Adam's work – the Fort Knox interior, the volcano rocket base and the oil tanker interior.

Adam was nominated for an Oscar for his work on *The Spy Who Loved Me*.

AD-LIB ANTICS: Sean Connery and Roger Moore were not adverse to adding their own lines to the script. In *From Russia With Love*, Rosa Klebb (Lotte Lenya), the evil SPECTRE agent, is attempting to kill 007 with a poisoned knife in the toes of her shoes. Bond turns the tables on her and kills her, and adds, 'at least she had her kicks'.

An example of Roger Moore's wit is evident in *Octopussy*. Bond comes face to face with a tiger. 007 tells the animal 'Sit!', like Barbara Woodhouse, the British dog expert and television celebrity. Not surprisingly, audiences outside Britain did not understand the joke.

AGENTS: During the course of the series, Bond is helped by a variety of agents working for his own department or for the Secret Service of a friendly nation. Of the twenty agents who worked with 007, nine did not survive their missions. They were: Quarrel (John Kitzmiller) in *Dr No*; Kerim Bey (Pedro Armendariz) in *From Russia with Love*; Paula (Martine Beswick) in *Thunderball*; Henderson (Charles Gray) and Aki (Akiko Wakabayashi) in *You Only Live Twice*; Campbell (Bernard Horsfall) in *OHMSS*; Ferrara (John Moreno) in *For Your Eyes Only*; Vijay (Vijay Amritraj) in *Octopussy* and Sir Godfrey Tibbett (Patrick McNee) in *A View To A Kill*.

AKI: A liberated Japanese female of the sixties era, Aki (Akiko Wakabayashi) is an agent of the Japanese SIS in *You Only Live Twice*. Bond, who meets her at a Sumo wrestling match, grows genuinely fond of Aki. She saves him from the clutches of SPECTRE on numerous occasions – roaring to 007's rescue in a nippy Toyota 2000 sports car, registration number 20 – 00, equipped with radio and television connections to headquarters.

Aki suffers what many Bond fans believe is the series' most original death. She is poisoned by SPECTRE agents. The poison intended for Bond is lowered, drop by drop, down a length of string while the couple sleep side by side. Aki moves in her sleep and the deadly substance falls into her mouth by mistake.

MAJOR ANYA AMASOVA: Agent Triple X of the KGB and the Soviet Union's leading female agent, Major Amasova appears in *The Spy Who Loved Me*. She is, with the exception of Tracy (Diana Rigg) in *OHMSS*, the most vividly written and portrayed female role in the series. Played by American Actress Barbara Bach (now Mrs Ringo Starr), Anya is not only a match for Bond but on occasions takes the initiative from him.

Elegant but deadly, Anya is equally appealing in a revealing black evening dress or combat overall and uniform. She believes her gender is unimportant and strives to be any man's equal. She proudly tells 007 at one point: 'You don't have to worry about me, Commander – I went on a survival course to Siberia.' To which Bond replies, dryly: 'Yes, I believe a great number of your countrymen do.'

Anya is loyal, patriotic and loving. She discovers that Bond is responsible for the death of her lover Sergei (Michael Billington) and threatens revenge. 007 discovers her reloading her gun aboard the USS Wayne and flippantly asks which bullet has his name on it – the first or the last. Anya retorts, coldly: 'I've never failed on a mission, Commander . . . any mission.'

Agent Triple X drinks vodka on the rocks and has a special blend of cigarettes containing knockout gas instead of tobacco. The teaming of the British Secret Service and the KGB – 007 and Triple X – against a common foe, Karl Stromberg (Curt Jurgens), introduces an entirely new male/female relationship to the series.

AMERICAN AID: Although a British agent, Bond's film career has seen him heavily involved with working with the US Government. *Dr No* features a plot to damage space operations at Cape Canaveral, while two years later 007 was battling to prevent *Goldfinger* (Gert Frobe) detonating a nuclear device at Fort Knox.

Thunderball and *Diamonds Are Forever* see Bond thwarting SPECTRE plans to destroy major US cities. *Live and Let Die* centres around a scheme by Mr Big (Yaphet Kotto) to flood the US with heroin. *Octopussy* features 007 preventing the detonation of a nuclear weapon at a USAF air base in West Germany, while in *A View To A Kill*, Bond outwits Max Zorin (Christopher Walken) who plots the destruction of silicon valley in California.

ANDREA ANDERS: Mistress of Scaramanga (Christopher Lee), *The Man With The Golden Gun*, Andrea is played by Maud Adams. Miss Adams is the only female lead to appear in two Bond films. She also featured in *Octopussy*.

Miss Anders is bored with her lonely life with Scaramanga – a killer who makes love only before a kill. Her role is reduced to providing a mere release for him from his work. Moreover, Andrea is expected to run errands for Scaramanga. She collects the golden bullets made by Lazar (Marne Maitland). Such is Miss Anders' desire to escape, that she sends a golden bullet with 007 inscribed upon it to Bond. This, she hopes, will lure 007 to Scaramanga and lead to his death.

But Bond persuades Miss Anders to retrieve the Solex Agitator – so vital to Scaramanga's plans. Miss Anders promises delivery but before she can make contact with 007 she is killed by Scaramanga, 'a difficult but most gratifying shot'.

ASTON MARTIN: Vehicles furnished by luxury car makers Aston Martin feature in five Bond films: *Goldfinger, Thunderball, OHMSS, Diamonds Are Forever* and *The Living Daylights*. Cinema audiences were first introduced to 007's Aston Martin DB5 in *Goldfinger* and this was probably the most memorable car to appear in the series. The same vehicle features in *Thunderball*.

The DB5 was equipped with an impressive array of weapons and modifications which included front-wing machine guns, wheel scythes, a tracking device with an audio-visual range of 150 miles, smoke screen, oil slick facilities, rear bullet-proof screen, revolving number plates – valid in all countries – and an ejector seat.

The ejector seat was salvaged from a fighter plane and

could only be used in long shot as it took up so much room in the car. For close-up shots an ordinary passenger seat was used. In addition to the British number plate BMT 126A, the car also carried the registration numbers 4711-EA-62 and LV-6789.

A later model of the car – registration number GKX 8G – features in *OHMSS*. Apart from a concealed weapons compartment, there appeared to be no other special modifications. Tracy Bond (Diana Rigg) is killed by Irma Bunt (Ilse Steppat) while a passenger in the car on the Bonds' honeymoon.

The Aston Martin cars featured in the Bond series are now privately owned in the USA.

ATAC: The Automatic Targetting Attack Communicator fitted to the St George's – a British spyship disguised as a fishing vessel – is a device used, as Bond says 'as an ultra-low frequency coded transmitter to order our submarines to launch ballistic missiles'.

The accidental loss of the ATAC, at the beginning of *For Your Eyes Only*, is a matter of consternation for the Secret Service. Bill Tanner (James Villiers) points out that if the device was to fall into the wrong hands, not only could every order be countermanded, but 'our own submarines could be ordered to attack our cities'.

AVENGERS: The successful television adventure series of the 1960s, *The Avengers*, and its updated version in the 1970s, *The New Avengers*, has strong links with the Bond series. Three of the four leading ladies have appeared in the 007 series.

Honor Blackman moved from the leather-clad Cathy Gale to star as the equally tough Pussy Galore in *Goldfinger*. Diana Rigg, Emma Peel of *The Avengers*, became the ill-fated Tracy Bond in *OHMSS*. Also in the same film, Joanna Lumley, who played Purdey in *The New Avengers*, appeared as one of the girls at the Piz Gloria mountain top clinic.

Patrick MacNee, of John Steed fame in the original and later series, featured as Sir Godfrey Tibbett, spy and racehorse trainer, in *A View To A Kill*.

BAD HABITS: Monks from the 600-year-old Meteora monastery in Greece, where the climax of *For Your Eyes Only* was filmed, were angry about the use of such a holy place in the picture. In protest they hung out dirty washing in an attempt to spoil the film crew's shots. The monks were apparently unhappy about James Bond's reputation for sex and violence.

BARON SAMEDI: Voodoo god and chief of the Legion of the Dead in *Live And Let Die* is Baron Samedi (Geoffrey Holder). He is a mysterious villain and his role in the film is never fully explained. Baron Samedi appears to be a nightclub entertainer performing for foreign tourists in the expensive hotels of San Monique. And yet we learn he is an associate of Mr Big (Yaphet Kotto), used to frighten gangsters and islanders on the heroin-producing island.

The announcer of Baron Samedi's act claims that the character is 'the man who cannot die'. The script shies away from answering questions on this most enigmatic Bondian villain apart from a nicely judged last glimpse of the character. In a final hand-to-hand encounter with Bond at the voodoo ceremony on San Monique, Baron Samedi is tossed into a coffin containing deadly snakes. Briefly, he writhes in agony before lying still – presumably dead.

But the last shot in *Live And Let Die*, after Bond has disposed of Tee-Hee (Julian W. Harris) – supposedly the last remaining member of Mr Big's organisation – aboard a train, Baron Samedi is seen riding on the front of the engine, raising his hat and laughing cruelly. Such is the power of Geoffrey Holder's performance that this makes a chilling end to the film.

JOHN BARRY: Composer John Barry has been connected with the series for twenty-five years. Barry arranged the original Bond theme which has become indelibly linked with the character.

Barry composed the scores for eleven subsequent 007 adventures: *From Russia With Love*, *Goldfinger*, *Thunderball*, *You Only Live Twice*, *OHMSS*, *Diamonds Are Forever*, *The Man With The Golden Gun*, *Moonraker*, *Octopussy*, *A View To A Kill* and *The Living Daylights*. His name has been missing from three Bonds: *Live And Let Die*, scored by George Martin; *The Spy Who Loved Me*, scored by Marvin Hamlisch and *For Your Eyes Only*, written by Bill Conti.

Barry has said of his work on Bond films: 'The films put forth a kind of simple, almost endearing, comic-strip attitude towards danger, intrigue and romance. But the main theme is to carry it off with style. Don't belittle the subject matter or make it cheap. Just give it a lot of style and make it sound like a million dollars.'

Yorkshire-born Barry began his work with British big bands and went on to form his own musical group, The John Barry Seven. Among the other films he has worked on are *Zulu*, *The Ipcress File*, *King Rat*, *The Wrong Box*, *Midnight Cowboy* and *The Black Hole*. He has received four Academy Awards: *The Lion in Winter* (best score), *Born Free* (best score and best song) and *Out of Africa* (best score).

RUBY BARTLETT: One of Blofeld's 'Angels of Death' in *OHMSS* is Ruby Bartlett (Angela Scoular) from Morecambe Bay, Lancashire. She is the first of the girls at Blofeld's allergy clinic in Switzerland to be bedded by Bond who is in the guise of Sir Hilary Bray (George Baker).

Ruby is the daughter of a chicken farmer and has gone to the clinic to be cured of an allergy to chickens. She explains to Bond that this used to make her break out all over and adds, 'you'd be surprised where'.

SHIRLEY BASSEY: International singing star Shirley Bassey is the only recording artist to sing more than one title song in the 007 series. She sang the title songs to *Goldfinger*, *Diamonds Are Forever* and *Moonraker*. All the numbers take the same title as the films.

Goldfinger was written by John Barry, Leslie Bricusse and Anthony Newley. There were good sales of the record on both sides of the Atlantic. Miss Bassey often uses the number to introduce her act.

Diamonds Are Forever was written by John Barry and Don Black. *Moonraker* saw Barry teaming up with Hal David to write the song.

BATMAN: After Sean Connery relinquished the role of 007 following *You Only Live Twice*, Adam West, star of the popular American television series *Batman*, was among the names mentioned as the new Bond in *OHMSS*, the next film. Hollywood stars Richard Burton and Lee Marvin were also said to be in contention for the role. In the end it went to little-known Australian actor, George Lazenby.

BATHOSUB: Bond's arch-rival Blofeld (Charles Gray) in *Diamonds Are Forever* has a one-man submarine, a Bathosub, on standby in the event of danger at his oil rig headquarters.

BEACH LIFE: Beaches have provided the background to several Bond sequences of action and romance. In *Dr No*, Bond, Honey (Ursula Andress) and Quarrel (John Kitzmiller) are fired upon by *Dr No*'s (Joseph Wiseman) high-powered launch.

OHMSS sees Bond's first meeting with Tracy (Diana Rigg) on a beach. This is marred by having to fight off two tough gangsters employed by Tracy's father, Marc-Ange Draco (Gabriele Ferzetti).

In *The Spy Who Loved Me*, Bond and Anya Amasova (Barbara Bach) drive out of the sea on to a crowded beach by means of the specially adapted Lotus Esprit. The vehicle transforms itself into a submarine. *For Your Eyes Only* sees Bond and Lisl (Cassandra Harris) attacked by Dune buggies on a beach – an attack which leaves Lisl dead.

Romance blossomed on the beach for Bond. Honey emerged from the sea on the beaches of Crab Key to the surprised 007. There was a love-making scene on the sand between Bond and Domino (Claudine Auger) in *Thunderball*. The situation was a beach in the Bahamas.

Miami Beach features in two consecutive films. It provides a background to the first meeting between 007 and Goldfinger (Gert Frobe) in *Goldfinger*. The beach is the target for the first SPECTRE-stolen atomic bomb in *Thunderball*.

BECHMANN AND MARKOVITZ: Dr Bechmann (Cyril Shaps) and Professor Markovitz (Milo Sperber) are the scientists who developed the submarine tracking system used by Karl Stromberg (Curt Jurgens) in *The Spy Who Loved Me*. For their work, Stromberg promised each ten million dollars but he reneges on the deal by killing them. A bomb is planted in the duo's helicopter when their work is completed.

BERETTA .25: Bond's gun from the early novels is mentioned only once in the film series, at the initial M/Bond scene in *Dr No*.

We learn that the Beretta jammed on Bond during his last mission and that he spent six months on sick leave as a result. It is because of this that M orders Bond to switch to the famous Walther PPK, with which he has been armed ever since.

BEST BELUGA: Always with a liking for the finer things in life, Bond has consumed Beluga caviar on three occasions in the series. He treats himself and Domino (Claudine Auger) to Dom Perignon '55 and Beluga caviar during his stay in the Bahamas during the *Thunderball* case. He helps himself to a generous spoonful of the delicacy as a reward for fighting off an attacker in Tracy's (Diana Rigg) room in *OHMSS*. The Siberian pre-credits sequence from *A View To A Kill* has 007 escaping to the West with a microchip, a bottle of vodka, 'rather shaken', and a supply of Beluga.

KERIM BEY: The smoking, drinking, womanising head of Station T Turkey, Kerim Bey (Pedro Armendariz), is M's (Bernard Lee) highly respected agent in Istanbul who masquarades as a carpet seller. This gregarious gypsy of a character is featured in *From Russia With Love*. Bey has a large family working as agents in the city, 'the biggest family pay-roll in Turkey'.

His daily exercise, at eleven in the morning and three in the afternoon, is to take a punt through the sewers and underground drains of Istanbul to a spot beneath the Soviet Embassy. Here he has the use of a Royal Navy periscope and is able to spy on the activities of the Soviets.

Sadly, Armendariz was dying of cancer during the filming and some of his scenes with Connery were shot with Connery in close-up and director Terence Young standing in for Armendariz. While lying seriously ill in Los Angeles hospital a month before shooting was to be completed, Armendariz took his own life.

BIANCA: Bond's helper in the South American pre-credits sequence in *Octopussy* is Bianca (Tina Hudson). Tina, a model, has another claim to fame. She once featured in Britain's first 'live' advertising poster. Instead of just appearing in a picture, she posed in the poster in person – creating much more than a 3-D effect.

BIG MOUTH: *From Russia With Love* sees Bond and Kerim Bey (Pedro Armendariz) tail a Soviet agent, Krilencu (Fred Haggerty), through the streets of Istanbul. He is cornered in a house with a large film advertisement on one side of the building. The advertisement is for a film starring Bob Hope and Anita Ekberg entitled *Call Me Bwana*, produced by Harry Saltzman and Cubby Broccoli. Krilencu tries to escape through the window on the side of the building – it appears as if he is emerging from Anita Ekberg's mouth – but he is shot dead by Kerim Bey.

MAURICE BINDER: Title designer for all but two Bond films, *From Russia With Love* and *Goldfinger*, Maurice Binder is renowned for his innovative designs featuring tasteful nudes and striking effects. Binder began by designing advertisements and catalogues for Macys, the US chain of department stores, during the 1940s.

COUNT DE BLEAUCHAMP: Blofeld lays claim to the heraldic title of Count De Bleauchamp in *OHMSS*. Sir Hilary Bray (George Baker) of the College of Arms, London, tells 007 that the real De Bleauchamps originated from Augsburg. Bond muses that inviting Blofeld to the family tombs would be one way of winkling the villain out of the relative safety of Switzerland. Bond travels to the continent, impersonating Sir Hilary, and invites De Bleauchamp to the tombs at Augsburg Cathedral. This is a serious error as the tombs are at the St Anna Kirche. 'A small slip,' Blofeld (Telly Savalas) notes, but one large enough to blow Bond's cover as Sir Hilary Bray.

A trait of the De Bleauchamp family is that they all lack ear lobes. And, sure enough, Blofeld has none. But 007 comments that it would take more than the cutting off of his ear lobes to make Blofeld a legitimate count.

BLEAUCHAMP INSTITUTE: Blofeld's (Telly Savalas) allergy research clinic atop Piz Gloria in Switzerland is called the Bleauchamp Institute. This is where his 'Angels Of Death' are being prepared to spread bacteriological warfare agents around the world. It is done under the guise of the girls being prepared for allergy cures.

The real-life location of the Bleauchamp Institute in *OHMSS* is the restaurant complex at the summit of

Mount Schilthorn in the Swiss Alps, 10,000 feet above sea level.

BLEEKER FLYING SCHOOL: Situated at Lake Front Airport, New Orleans, the Bleeker Flying School is touched by the Bondian world in dramatic fashion. 007, fleeing Mr Big's (Yaphet Kotto) heavies in this scene from *Live And Let Die*, commandeers a Cessna trainer – number N 77029 – with a pupil waiting in the aircraft for a lesson, Mrs Bell (Ruth Kempf).

BLOFELD: A sadist who repays failure with death and an extortionist who will renege on a deal at will, Ernst Stavro Blofeld is the founder of SPECTRE and Bond's arch enemy for many adventures in the series. Blofeld is played by Anthony Dawson in *From Russia With Love* (Eric Pohlmann provides the voice), Donald Pleasence in *You Only Live Twice*, Telly Savalas in *OHMSS* and Charles Gray in *Diamonds Are Forever*. The unseen Blofeld in *Thunderball* was given the voice of actor Joseph Wiseman, 007's first screen foe, Dr No.

Blofeld is an animal lover. His constant companion is a white cat and he has a penchant for bizarre fish. Siamese fighting fish in *From Russia With Love* and piranha fish in *You Only Live Twice*. Blofeld smokes and wears the SPECTRE ring on the little finger of his right hand.

One reason why he may have stayed one step ahead of the authorities is his constant change of appearance. Thus the 'scarred, asexual monster' of *You Only Live Twice* becomes a charming, witty cad in *Diamonds Are Forever*.

BLOODLESS: The film *Goldfinger* sees the emergence of stylised violence in the series. Despite the large number of fatalities in the picture, there is not a single drop of blood spilt.

BOAT BLOW: Roger Moore's debut as 007 in *Live And Let Die* was marred by an accident he suffered two days before cameras started rolling. While rehearsing a fifteen-minute speedboat chase – a highlight of the film – his vessel collided with a large corrugated iron building jutting out from a Louisiana Bayou.

BOBSLEIGH: Two Bond films feature bobsleighs. *OHMSS* has a thrillingly-staged climax – Bond chasing Blofeld (Telly Savalas). Eventually they end up fighting in Blofeld's sleigh.

In *For Your Eyes Only*, Bond, while attempting to ski his way out of being run down by Kriegler (John Wyman) on a motor-cycle, skis on to a bobsleigh run and finds himself behind a four-man bobsleigh team.

But tragically, during the filming of this stunt, a sleigh overturned killing one of the occupants. This is one of the few accidents suffered in the course of making Bond films.

WILLY BOGNER JNR: World-class champion skier Willy Bogner has provided an enormous amount of excitement in the series in his staging and filming of snow scenes. Bogner's first link comes in *OHMSS* when he photographs not only the ski chases but also the bobsleigh climax by ski-ing backwards with a hand-held camera to capture the action.

In addition to providing the same facilities during the filming of *For Your Eyes Only*, his company also provided the ski suits for cast and crew. Roger Moore sports a Bogner-designed jacket during the Cortina sequences.

Bogner is also credited as ski sequence director and photographer in *A View To A Kill*. The pre-credit sequences feature a ski chase. Bond is also pursued on a snow mobile by a Soviet helicopter and this culminates in 007 having to resort to snow surfing on one of the runners from the wrecked snow mobile to effect his escape. A superb sequence.

During the pre-credits sequence of *A View To A Kill* Roger Moore wears clothes designed by Bogner.

TRACY BOND: Countess Teresa di Vicenzo (Diana Rigg), daughter of Marc-Ange Draco (Gabriele Ferzetti), and an Englishwoman who ventured into the mountains looking for bandits, is the most important female character in the series. She appears in *OHMSS* and becomes the first, and so far only, Mrs Bond.

Born in 1943, Tracy's first appearance in the film is far from promising. 007 is called upon to save her from a suicide attempt. Tracy is burning herself out. She is part of the international jet set, jumping from one scandal to another. A disastrous marriage to an Italian count hardly helped matters – he killed himself in a Mazerati with one of his mistresses – and she is bent on a course of self-destruction.

Her father believes that a relationship between 007 and Tracy would solve his daughter's problems. At first, Bond is reluctant, but they gradually fall in love and marry.

Tracy has a strong personality and, like Bond, enjoys the good things of life. She drives a red Cougar sports car with French number plates, registration 23IB TT75.

She dies at the hands of Irma Bunt (Ilse Steppat), Blofeld's (Telly Savalas) assistant, just hours after her wedding to Bond. She is buried at Stoke Poges, Buckinghamshire, England. Bond is seen placing flowers at her grave at the beginning of *For Your Eyes Only*. Tracy is also briefly referred to by Major Anya Amasova (Barbara Bach) in *The Spy Who Loved Me*.

BONDIAN HYPE: Advertising posters for the Bond films often incorporate a slogan for publicity purposes.

Dr No	– 'The First James Bond Film!'
From Russia With Love	– 'James Bond Is Back!'
Goldfinger	– 'James Bond Back In Action!'
Thunderball	– 'Look Up! Look Down! Look Out!

	Here Comes The Biggest Bond Of All!'
You Only Live Twice	– '... And Twice Is The Only Way To Live!'
OHMSS	– 'Far Up! Far Out! Far More! James Bond 007 Is Back!'
The Spy Who Loved Me	– 'It's The Biggest! It's The Best! It's Bond And Beyond!'
Moonraker	– 'Now Outer Space Belongs To James Bond!'
Octopussy	– 'James Bond's All Time High!'
A View To A Kill	– 'Has James Bond Finally Met His Match?'

The poster for *Live And Let Die* displayed a knife in place of the 'i' in 'Die'. The 'teaser' poster for *Octopussy* – the thirteenth in the official series and produced in competition with the Connery comeback, *Never Say Never Again* – read 'Nobody Does Him Better – Thirteen Times Better.' A slogan coined for a *A View To A Kill* but not used on the final poster was 'Adventure Above And Beyond All Other Bonds.'

BOOK-OF-THE-FILM: The trend of the late 1970s and 1980s of writing original novels based on film scripts caught up with the Bond series in 1977 and 1979.

Christopher Wood, co-writer of *The Spy Who Loved Me* and sole writer credited with the script for *Moonraker*, wrote two novelisations of the two scripts with which he was involved. Thus, in addition to Ian Fleming's original novels entitled *Moonraker* and *The Spy Who Loved Me*, *Moonraker* and *The Spy Who Loved Me* appeared as books-of-the-films under Christopher Wood's authorship.

MAJOR BOOTHROYD: Popularly referred to as 'Q', Major Boothroyd is the British Secret Service gadget inventor and he has developed into one of the most enjoyable characters of the series. Boothroyd's debut in the series – sketched by actor Peter Burton – is in *Dr No*. The character has appeared in every subsequent Bond film with the exception of *Live And Let Die*.

In *From Russia With Love*, the part was taken by Desmond Llewelyn and he has portrayed the character since that picture. Veteran actor Llewelyn made his movie debut in 1939 in a Will Hay comedy. His appearance as 'Q' in *The Living Daylights* means that Llewelyn has played opposite all four 007 stars.

On screen, 'Q' has equipped Bond with everything in gadgetry from television wrist watches to underwater sports cars. But in real life, Llewelyn is less efficient with electronic items. It is said he once had to request help when using a bank's cash dispenser.

It was decided by director Terence Young that the character of 'Q' in *From Russia With Love* should be played by Llewelyn in a straight fashion. This concept has evolved over the years to such an extent that 'Q' is now the straight man for Bond to bounce his jokes off.

Through Llewelyn's deadpan portrayal of Boothroyd, the character has become an essential part of the series. The advent of each new Bond promises yet more gadgets from this likeable magician of the 20th century.

BOTTOMS UP: The sequence in *Dr No* when Professor Dent (Anthony Dawson) attempts to kill Bond by placing a poisonous spider in 007's bed reveals that Bond sleeps in blue pyjama bottoms. In *Goldfinger*, during the Miami sequences, Jill Masterson (Shirley Eaton) wears the top half of a pair of blue pyjamas. Bond wears the other half.

BOTTOMS UP CLUB: The Bottoms Up Club in Hong Kong,

a bar and strip joint, is a killing ground for Scaramanga (Christopher Lee) in *The Man With The Golden Gun*. Missing solar energy expert Gibson is shot while being escorted from the club by Lieutenant Hip (Soon-Taik-Oh). This is witnessed by 007 who has been searching for Gibson's solar cell data.

BOXING CLEVER: In three films, telephones have provided a background for Bondian action. In *Thunderball*, Bond's call to headquarters about the Tong sign tattooed on Count Lippe's (Guy Doleman) wrist is overheard by Lippe himself, outside the telephone booth. This forces Lippe to take drastic measures to eliminate Bond. 007's frantic efforts to thwart the detonation of a nuclear device in *Octopussy* grind to a halt when the telephone box he wishes to use is hogged by a talkative woman.

The most dramatic telephone box sequence happens in *OHMSS*. 007 attempts to telephone through to headquarters and is shot by SPECTRE agents in the process. The gun fire, the glass shattering and Bond's flight to the relative safety of Tracy's (Diana Rigg) red Cougar car raises the curtain on one of the series' most outrageous but entertaining car chases.

SIR HILARY BRAY: Bond assumes the identity of Sir Hilary Bray (George Baker), an official of the College of Arms in London, in *OHMSS*. He does so in an attempt to trap Blofeld (Telly Savalas) who has taken up residence in Switzerland and has contacted the College of Arms to confirm his claim to the heraldic title of Count de Bleauchamp. George Baker returns to the series in *The Spy Who Loved Me* as Captain Benson.

BRIEF ENCOUNTER: Did Ian Fleming ever appear in a Bond film? Judging from careful viewings of the Orient Express sequences in *From Russia With Love*, it is almost certain that the figure standing by the side of the railway-track in one shot is the writer himself.

During the shooting of the film, various publicity stills were taken of Fleming watching the film-makers. He was wearing a white sweater and grey trousers. He carried a walking stick. The description matches perfectly that of the character standing by the railway track during the external shot of the Orient Express rushing past just after the death of Kerim Bey (Pedro Armendrariz).

MISS BRINK: Former world class ice-skater Miss Brink (Jill Bennett), whose previous triumphs have been witnessed by James Bond, is employed by Kristatos (Julian Glover) in *For Your Eyes Only* to train his young protégé Bibi Dahl (Lynn-Holly Johnson) to win a gold medal in the Winter Olympics.

But Kristatos announces his attention to take Miss Brink and Bibi to Cuba and they decide to leave him. Miss Brink goes to Bond and his associates for help at the climax of the film.

CUBBY BROCCOLI: Albert Romolo Broccoli has produced all fifteen Bond films, from *Dr No* to *The Living Daylights*, since securing the finance for the project with Harry Saltzman from United Artists in 1961.

Broccoli produced the first nine films in partnership with Saltzman. Between them they formed Eon Productions. When Saltzman sold his interest to United Artists, Broccoli became the sole producer and his first Bond solo was *The Spy Who Loved Me*, released in 1977.

His film career began as an assistant director under director Howard Hawks working on *The Outlaw*. His first film as a producer was on *Red Beret*, starring Alan Ladd, in 1953.

Broccoli, whose Italian family lent its name to the vegetable of the same name which they introduced to America, has enjoyed a long and highly memorable film career. In addition to creating the screen exploits of 007, his charitable work for the needy has been unstinting.

BROCCOLI ON BOND: 'What makes Bond is beautiful girls, action and a good story.' *Producer Cubby Broccoli, June 1981.*

PIERCE BROSNAN: When, after seven films, Roger Moore retired from the role of 007, the hunt was on for a new Bond. Eon Productions looked towards Irish actor Pierce Brosnan, star of the television detective series Remington Steel. The producers wanted Brosnan and the actor was keen to become the next Bond. But there were contractual difficulties and the makers of Remington Steel refused to release Brosnan.

With only weeks to go before the start on the next Bond film, *The Living Daylights*, Eon Productions were in a tight corner. But after casting their eye over a number of hopefuls, Eon plumped for British actor Timothy Dalton, famed for his Shakespearian roles.

BUDGET BLOCKBUSTER: The final budget for *Moonraker* released in 1979 was more than thirty million dollars. This total exceeded the cost of the first eight 007 films put together.

BUGGING: Bugging devices, supplied by Q-Branch, have been used by Bond in several films. The first occasion is in *Goldfinger* when two models, a magnetised version roughly the size of a cigarette packet and a smaller version that fits in the heel of Bond's shoe, are used by 007 in his fight against Auric Goldfinger (Gert Frobe).

In *Thunderball*, Bond is issued with a radioactive pill, said to be harmless, which must be swallowed to allow a signal to be transmitted. In *OHMSS* (Desmond Llewelyn) develops 'radioactive lint' which, if placed in an opponent's pocket, will allow a locational fix to be kept.

Bugging devices also appear in *The Man With The Golden Gun* and *Octopussy*. Mary Goodnight (Britt Ekland) has a dress fitted with a homer in the bottom and also uses a homer, similar to the one used by 007 in *Goldfinger*, to track Scaramanga's (Christopher Lee) car.

In *Octopussy*, the fake Fabergé egg with which the Secret Service aims to infiltrate Prince Kamal Khan's (Louis Jourdan) organisation is fitted with a tiny bugging device which is compatible with a receiver in Bond's watch.

IRMA BUNT: Irma Bunt, short, squat and stocky, is the female wardress and assistant to Ernst Stavro Blofeld at the SPECTRE allergy clinic of Piz Gloria, Switzerland. Bunt is played by Ilse Steppat in *OHMSS*, her only appearance in the movie series – the character was in two of the Bond novels.

Irma Bunt deserves special remembrance from Bond fans in that it was she, and not Blofeld as commonly believed, who fired the fatal shots at Tracy (Diana Rigg), Bond's wife of less than a day, at the tragic conclusion of *OHMSS*.

C & W INCORPORATED: Carlos and Wilmsberg are a Rio De Janeiro import-export firm with a warehouse at Carioca Avenue. The business features in *Moonraker*. A subsidiary of Drax Group, C & W Incorporated is used by Hugo Drax (Michael Lonsdale) to help transport his globes containing nerve gas from their Venetian origins to the space shuttles for use in Operation Orchard.

CABINET SECRET: A Government filing cabinet situated in Miss Moneypenny's (Lois Maxwell) office hides one of her beauty secrets. In *OHMSS* she asks Bond how he expects a girl to 'keep herself alluring'. A scene from *For Your Eyes Only* provides the answer. Pull out a drawer and an electronic mirror, fitted by 'Q' (Desmond Llewelyn) no doubt, pops up along with a supply of lipsticks. This enables Moneypenny to add the finishing touches to her make-up just in time for Bond's arrival at headquarters. This prompts him to comment that she is a 'feast for my eyes'.

CABLE CARS: Cable cars have added excitement to two Bond films in the series. In *OHMSS* Bond breaks out of his prison in Blofeld's (Telly Savalas) Alpine allergy clinic by edging perilously along a cable car cable. Bond is almost run down by the advancing car – escaping only by dropping onto the car roof.

In *Moonraker*, Bond and CIA agent Holly Goodhead (Lois Chiles) are attacked by massive steel-toothed assassin, Jaws (Richard Kiel), while descending in a large cable car from the top of Rio's Sugar Loaf mountain. The fight between Bond and Jaws takes them on to the windswept roof of the cable car. Bond and Holly make their escape from their attacker by throwing a chain round the cable and sliding down to safety.

SYD CAIN: Former RAF pilot Syd Cain has worked with Cubby Broccoli since before the formation of Eon Productions. Cain was production designer on three Bonds: *From Russia With Love*, *OHMSS* and *Live And Let Die*.

CAMEO ROLES: Several famous actors and celebrities have appeared as minor characters in cameo roles. Anthony Dawson, of Professor Dent fame in *Dr No*, features unseen as Blofeld in *From Russia With Love*. Joseph Wiseman, who played Dr No, provides the voice of Blofeld in *Thunderball*. Veteran screen villain Eric Pohlmann was the voice of Blofeld in *From Russia With Love*. The production manager on *From Russia With Love*, Bill Hill, portrayed the character Captain Nash in the same film. Michael Wilson, scriptwriter and latterly co-producer of the series, was an American tourist in *Octopussy* and veteran British comedian Alfie Bass played a consumptive Italian in the Venetian sequences of *Moonraker*.

Legend has it that Sammy Davis Jr contributed a cameo appearance in *Diamonds Are Forever* but that short sequence was later edited out. Several newspapers in 1983 speculated that Roger Moore was to make an appearance in the Connery comeback, *Never Say Never Again*, but nothing came of this.

CAMPUS CHAT: After the filming of *From Russia With Love* in 1963, Sean Connery was nominated for election as Rector of St Andrew's University, Scotland, along with Julius Nyerere and Peter Ustinov. Connery felt honoured that he should be chosen but unfortunately he was not elected.

PAULA CAPLAN: Bond's secret service aid in Nassau on the Thunderball mission, Paula Caplan (Martine Beswick), commits suicide rather than answer questions from SPECTRE when she is captured. Martine previously appeared in *From Russia With Love* in the role of Zora.

CAR CHASES: A staple ingredient of most action films, a car chase, has featured in all but two movies in the series. The exceptions are *From Russia With Love* and *Moonraker*. The most memorable is surely in *Diamonds Are Forever* when 007 and Tiffany Case (Jill St John) are chased by what seems to be the entire Las Vegas police force. Stunt arrangers Bob Simmons and Paul Baxley ensured that Bond tipped his car on two wheels to escape his pursuers by squeezing through the narrow exit at the end of the alleyway.

Perhaps the most ridiculous is in *You Only Live Twice* when the car pursuing Bond and Aki (Akiko Wakabayashi) is lifted off the road by a giant magnet suspended beneath a helicopter. The vehicle is released into the sea.

The first car chase is in *Dr No* on the way to Kingston Airport. This first-class action sequence is followed by the first fight.

CARNIVAL!: On three occasions 007 has been chased through a happy throng of carnival revellers by minor villains intent on murder. The combination of merry celebrations and violence is a potent one. Bond is chased through a traditional Junkanoo procession in *Thunderball*. On his trail is Fiona (Luciana Paluzzi) and a handful of SPECTRE agents. This sequence marks the only occasion when 007 is shot and wounded. When Fiona and her men lose Bond's trail they follow the trail of blood he is leaving.

Having escaped the Alpine fortress of Blofeld (Telly Savalas) by means of skis in *OHMSS*, Bond is forced to gatecrash a Christmas party in a Swiss village. He is almost run to ground amid the celebrations until the unexpected appearance of Tracy (Diana Rigg) paves the way to his escape.

In *Moonraker*, Bond and Manuela (Emily Bolton), a British agent assigned to Station VH, are attacked by Jaws (Richard Kiel) at carnival time in Rio.

MISS CARUSO: Italian secret agent Miss Caruso (Madeline Smith) is the first woman that Roger Moore as 007 makes love to on screen. She is featured in *Live And Let Die* and we are told she helped 007 on a secret mission. The Italian secret service, though pleased with Bond's work, are worried by the disappearance of agent Caruso after the mission. This is solved when she is seen in bed with Bond at 007's flat.

ROSIE CARVER: Ostensibly a CIA agent, Rosie Carver (Gloria Henry) is a double working also for Mr Big (Yaphet Kotto) in *Live And Let Die*. She delivers Bond into Mr Big's clutches on the island of San Monique. A Tarot card informs 007 that he is dealing with a woman who is a 'liar and a cheat'. For her duplicity Bond is ruthless but still takes time to make love to her. She claims he would not kill her after their lovemaking but 007 snaps back, 'I certainly wouldn't have killed you before'.

Rosie dies at the hands of her employer, Mr Big. She is shot when it seems she is about to crack in the face of Bond's questioning. The love scene between Moore and Gloria Hendry was shot at the same location in Jamaica used for the scenes involving Sean Connery and Ursula Andress in the Crab Key sequences of *Dr No*.

TIFFANY CASE: Miss Case, played with supreme coolness by Jill St John, is the female lead of *Diamonds Are Forever*, the Amsterdam link in the diamond smuggling pipeline stretching from South Africa to the USA. Bond is amused by Tiffany's name and she explains, 'I was born there, on the first floor, while my mother was looking for a wedding ring.' 'Well, I'm glad for your sake that it wasn't Van Cleef and Arpels,' replies Bond drily.

CASINO ROYALE: Two film versions of Fleming's first novel, *Casino Royale*, have been completed but neither involved Eon Productions. The US television network CBS produced an hour long version in 1954 with American actor Barry Nelson appearing as the first 007. Peter Lorre was the villain, le Chiffre and Linda Christian provided the female interest, but the feature was not a success.

Fleming sold the rights to the film to director Gregory Ratoff, who later disposed of them to producer Charles K. Feldman. Feldman was unable to secure Sean Connery who was under contract to Eon Productions, so he opted to produce *Casino Royale* as a huge spoof of the Bond series which at that time, 1966–67, was reaching a peak.

With an all-star cast which included David Niven – reputedly Fleming's personal choice to play 007 – as Sir James Bond, Peter Sellers, Woody Allen, Deborah Kerr, Orson Welles, John Huston (in a red wig as 'M') and Ursula Andress, three credited script writers and six credited directors, Huston among them, the film was little more than an expensive mess.

'One of the most shameless wastes of time and talent in screen history,' was the view of authoritative cinema expert, Leslie Halliwell. Only the score emerged with any credit. *The Look Of Love*, written by Burt Bacharach and Hal David, was nominated for an Oscar.

CAVENDISH: Hugo Drax's (Michael Lonsdale) English butler in *Moonraker* is Cavendish, played by Arthur

Howard. Cavendish is employed at the authentic French château in California's desert wastes. Arthur Howard is the brother of former British screen star Leslie Howard.

CENTRIFUGE TRAINER: Hugo Drax (Michael Lonsdale) in *Moonraker* makes use of a centrifuge trainer at his space shuttle complex in California. The machine is used in the training of space personnel to simulate the forces felt above our atmosphere. NASA-trained astronaut Holly Goodhead (Lois Chiles) explains to Bond that the machine can reach twenty Gs but this would be fatal. Three Gs is the equivalent of take-off pressure and most people pass out at seven. She adds, when 007 appears to be apprehensive at trying out the device, that a 70-year-old is capable of withstanding three Gs.

When Bond's session on the centrifuge trainer is sabotaged by Drax's assassin Chang (Toshiro Suga), the British agent manages to withstand thirteen Gs before halting the machine by means of an explosive dart from a wrist gun supplied to him by 'Q' earlier in the film.

CHARLIE: CIA driver Charlie in *Live And Let Die* collects Bond in a yellow taxi, registration number 545 BBB, on his arrival at New York's Kennedy Airport. Charlie is played by Joey Chitwood – one of the stunt co-ordinators working on the film.

CHEERS: Bond's favourite tipple is champagne which he drinks in every film except *Diamonds Are Forever*. The early releases show 007 having a liking for Dom Perignon. He enjoys a '55 in *Dr No* but expresses a preference for a '53, which he drinks in *Goldfinger*. Bond goes for a Dom Perignon '59 in *You Only Live Twice* and a '57 in *OHMSS*. *The Man With The Golden Gun* sees Bond opt for a '64, but he expresses a preference for a '62 and in *The Spy Who Loved Me* he tastes the delights of Dom Perignon '52.

Since *Moonraker* in 1979, Bond has insisted on Bollinger champagne. He samples a '69 with Holly Goodhead in

Moonraker and goes on to try a '75 in *A View To A Kill*.

From Russia With Love features 007 and Sylvia Trench (Eunice Gayson) drinking champagne aboard a punt. Bond chills the sparkling wine in the water by tying the bottle to his big toe and dropping the champagne over the side.

CHITTY CHITTY BANG BANG: Cubby Broccoli has produced a non-Bond book written by Ian Fleming for the big screen, *Chitty Chitty Bang Bang*. This popular children's fantasy was released in 1968. Film-makers associated with the Bond series helped to bring *Chitty Chitty Bang Bang* to the cinema and they included a set-designer, Ken Adam. Gert Frobe, who had previously played Auric Goldfinger in the Bond series, turned in a performance as a villain of the peace.

CHRISTMAS: The festive season is featured several times in the series. In *OHMSS* Bond, disguised as Sir Hilary Bray, arrives at Blofeld's (Telly Savalas) allergy research institute in Switzerland in the days running up to Christmas. As might be expected there are references to Christmas.

When Bond's true identity is discovered, he awakes after being knocked unconscious to find Blofeld putting the finishing touches to decorating a Christmas tree.

Blofeld's 'angels of death' – girls brainwashed into spreading biological warfare – are given special presents on leaving the institute on Christmas Eve: a make-up case consisting of an atomiser containing a biological virus and a powder compact which hides a powerful transmitter able to pick up Blofeld's brainwashing voice all over the world.

Other 007 films to have made passing references to the festive season include *From Russia With Love*. 'Q' (Desmond Llewelyn) supplies a gadget-ridden briefcase – with hidden knives and tear-gas cartridges – to Bond. 007 comments that the case is a 'nasty little Christmas present'.

In *Moonraker*, Bond is supplied with a wrist-gun capable of firing darts with armour-piercing or cyanide-dipped heads. Bond tells 'Q': 'You really must get them in the stores for Christmas.'

When, in *Diamonds Are Forever*, Bond is introduced to a voice box for disguising accents, 007 says to 'Q': 'You've surpassed yourself this time.' But 'Q' retorts, 'not a bit. I made one of these for the kids last Christmas.'

CIA: United States Central Intelligence Agency personnel regularly feature in Bond films and have helped 007 on some of his most perilous missions. Felix Leiter appears in five movies – *Dr No, Goldfinger, Thunderball, Diamonds Are Forever* and *Live And Let Die* – and the character has been played by Jack Lord, Cec Linder, Rick Van Nutter, Norman Burton and David Hedison.

Other CIA agents in the series include Rosie Carver (Gloria Hendry), a double agent in *Live And Let Die*; Holly Goodhead (Lois Chiles) in *Moonraker* and Chuck Lee (David Yip) in *A View To A Kill*. Rosie Carver and Chuck Lee are both killed but Holly Goodhead survives her mission.

We discover little about CIA activities. But in *Goldfinger* we find out the CIA agents' cars are fitted with identical homer screens and receivers, the same as those used by the British Secret Service. In *Thunderball*, Felix Leiter's equipment can pick up the signals sent out by the British homing pill swallowed by Bond.

The standard CIA weapon, according to Bond in *Live And Let Die*, is Smith and Wesson Custom 38 with a corrugated five-inch stock but no serial number. And the devious devices he discovers in Goodhead's bedroom in Venice – a ballpoint pen housing a poison-tipped needle, a diary firing a dart, a flame-thrower disguised as a scent bottle and handbag housing a radio transmitter – are all standard CIA equipment.

CLASSIC COCKTAIL: Surprisingly for a character so closely associated with such a classic cocktail, Bond consumes a

Vodka Martini shaken not stirred in only five films – *Dr No*, *Goldfinger*, *OHMSS*, *The Spy Who Loved Me* and *Moonraker*. Only once does 007 request the drink on screen and that is in *Goldfinger*.

CLEAN SCENE: The use of bathrooms has provided background detail to a variety of plot lines. Bathrooms feature twice as the backdrop for seduction scenes. Bond discovers SPECTRE killer Fiona (Luciana Paluzzi) in a bath during *Thunderball*. She asks 007 for something to wear... he hands her a pair of slippers.

Bond and Russian agent Pola Ivanova (Fiona Fullerton) meet each other while both are spying on Max Zorin's (Christopher Walken) oil plant near San Francisco in *A View To A Kill*. They retire to a nearby health spa to share a bath. Pola comments, 'détente is beautiful'.

But just as love can blossom in a bathroom, so can death strike. In the pre-credits sequence of *Goldfinger*, 007 dispatches an assassin into a bath. Bond kills an assailant by tossing an electric heater into the water. *Live And Let Die* see's 007's bathtime at his hotel chalet in the Caribbean spoiled by an unwelcome visitor. A snake emerges from the plumbing.

In *You Only Live Twice*, 007 is given special bathtime attention by Tiger Tanka's (Tetsuro Tamba) bikini-clad servants. And 007 is running a bath for himself in Istanbul when he discovers unwitting SPECTRE pawn, Tatiana Romanova (Daniella Bianchi), in his hotel bed, a memorable scene in *From Russia With Love*.

Perhaps the most impressive bathroom is to be found in the Whyte House of *Diamonds Are Forever*. Bond relaxes in a circular bath following his near-incineration in a crematorium.

There is much less action connected with shower cubicles. 007 and Honey (Ursula Andress) take a shower to rinse away radioactive dust in *Dr No*. Bond takes two showers in *A View To A Kill*, one following his bath with Pola and the other is shared with Stacey Sutton (Tanya Roberts).

CLOSE SHAVES: Bond is seen to have a moustache only once in the series, and then it is not a real one. 007 dons a false moustache in *Octopussy* in a sabotage mission in South America during the pre-credits sequence. The moustache helps to create a Latin American appearance. Bond is disguised as Colonel Toro, a South American officer.

COFFEE: Bond is a confirmed coffee addict. He drinks coffee with Honey (Ursula Andress) while in the clutches of Dr No (Joseph Wiseman). 007 orders a medium-sweet Turkish in *From Russia With Love* and the scenes of Bond's flat in *Live And Let Die* feature an intricate coffee-making machine. Bond makes a cup from the machine for 'M' (Bernard Lee). But when offered a cup of tea by Hugo Drax (Michael Lonsdale) in *Moonraker*, 007 declines the offer.

COLBY ON BOND: William Colby, head of the CIA from 1973–76, enjoys watching the exploits of 007. He once said that real spies were 'grey men in a crowd' and that he was puzzled how successful Bond was despite remaining most obtrusive. But William Colby adds: 'I am very glad that we have spies like Bond.'

COLLARED: When Bond is rescued in the snow by a St Bernard dog in *OHMSS* he expresses the hope that the beast is carrying a five-star Hennessey brandy. As in this instance, location has often dictated the drinking habits of the agent.

The Oriental flavour of *You Only Live Twice* enables 007 to sample the delights of Japanese saki and also endure the harshness of Siamese vodka. Bond is rather perplexed to be offered a Phuyuck '74 in *The Man With The Golden Gun*. While in *Goldfinger*, when in Kentucky, he comments that the bourbon and branch water is rather good in these parts. *Live And Let Die* sees 007 in New York where he opts for the bourbon and branch water.

Bond drinks scotch in *Dr No* but, while posing as Sir Hilary Bray in *OHMSS*, he orders a malt whisky, with none other than branch water.

Dining at the Bank of England with 'M' in *Goldfinger*, Bond is served a thirty-year-old 'indifferently' blended brandy.

Bond correctly identifies the vintage of a Solero sherry – based on the original vintage of 1851 – in *Diamonds Are Forever*. Later in the same film his knowledge of claret – a Mouton Rothschild '55 – blows the cover on fake waiters Mr Wint (Bruce Glover) and Mr Kidd (Putter Smith).

Mint juleps, though not too sweet, are the order of the day while staying with *Goldfinger* (Gert Frobe), and Felix Leiter (David Hedison) persuades 007 to order a similar drink in the New Orleans sequence of *Live And Let Die*.

COLLINS ON BOND: Film actress and Dynasty star Joan Collins once said of James Bond: 'I admire his style; his fast cars; his elegant clothes; the beautifully chilled bottle of Dom Perignon. For most women that is irresistible.'

MILOS COLUMBO: Known as The Dove, Columbo (Topol) is a mysterious Greek figure who becomes involved with Bond's mission in *For Your Eyes Only*. Columbo was once the inseparable ally of Kristatos (Julian Glover) and they fought together in the Greek wartime resistance against the Nazis. But since the war, both have been sworn enemies. Columbo joins forces with Bond to take on the might of Kristatos.

Columbo loses his mistress, Lisl (Cassandra Harris), to the agents of Kristatos in Corfu, but he is able to avenge her death by killing Kristatos at the film's conclusion.

Topol starred in *Fiddler On The Roof*.

COMMERCIAL TRAVELLER: Bond's patriotism does not extend to his choice of airlines. On only one occasion does 007 fly with a recognised British company. Bond's favourite airline appears to be Pan-Am. He flies courtesy of Pan-Am on three missions – *Dr No*, *From Russia With Love* and *Live And Let Die*. He chooses Lufthansa to travel from Amsterdam to Los Angeles in *Diamonds Are Forever* but flies with Apollo Airways in the pre-credits sequence of *Moonraker*. Arguably, 007's most spectacular journey is the trip from Europe to South America in *Moonraker*. On this occasion he flies Air France on board Concorde.

He makes an exception in *Goldfinger* by flying on British United Air Ferries in the pursuit of Goldfinger from Britain to Switzerland. 007's Aston Martin DB5 also makes the trip.

But, surprisingly, Bond is never seen to travel with 'the world's favourite airline,' British Airways.

SEAN CONNERY: Born on August 25th, 1930 in Edinburgh, Sean Connery was the cinema's first 007. Following a spell in the Royal Navy and representing Scotland in a Mr Universe contest, Connery began his acting career with a small part in a touring production of South Pacific. Stage, television and films followed and it was his appearance in the Walt Disney fantasy, *Darby O'Gill and the Little People*, that first brought Connery to the attention of Cubby Broccoli who, at that time in 1961, was searching for an actor to play Bond.

It has been claimed that Connery was paid just over twenty thousand pounds for his role in *Dr No*. Such was the success of the film that Connery returned to the role for *From Russia With Love*, *Goldfinger*, *Thunderball* and *You Only Live Twice*. After *You Only Live Twice* was released in 1967, Connery turned his back on the role. He vowed that he would never play Bond again. However, he was tempted back to play Bond in *Diamonds Are Forever*, released in 1971. Despite saying 'never again', he returned for one final fling for a non-Eon Bond film in 1983, aptly titled *Never Say Never Again*.

CRAB KEY: A fictitious island off Jamaica where Dr No's complex is based in Crab Key. The island boasts a nuclear power station and bauxite mine. The power station is used to topple American missiles launched from Cape Canaveral.

CRAPS: A dice game played by Bond at the Whyte House Casino in *Diamonds Are Forever* is craps. Despite winning fifty thousand dollars – fraudulently as it turns out – 007 confesses that he has played the game only once before. Plenty O'Toole (Lana Wood) cannot believe it. She tells Bond: 'You handled those cubes like a monkey handles coconuts.'

CRASH BASH: Bond and Pussy Galore (Honor Blackman) survive a plane crash at the climax of *Goldfinger*. This is the first of three such incidents from which 007 survives. Bond and Pussy take to a parachute to jump clear of the stricken plane heading speedily to earth.

In *You Only Live Twice*, Bond escapes a trap set by Helga (Karin Dor) who leaves him wedged in his seat. But he survives by leaping clear of the stricken plane. *Octopussy* sees 007 taking to the outside of an aircraft in his bid to stop Kamal Khan (Louis Jourdan) from escaping. Bond forces the plane to land by interfering with the engine and the wing flaps. The aircraft disappears over a cliff top but 007 throws himself clear in the nick of time.

CREDIT THIS: In the credits sequence in *Goldfinger*, scenes from the film are projected on to a static, gold-painted body of a model. Jill Masterson, played by popular British actress Shirley Eaton, is killed in a similar manner later on in the film but we are not told if it is Eaton who appears in the early sequence.

James Bond is glimpsed among the scenes. This is the first time that the actor playing Bond is seen in the credits sequence, but it is not the last. The silhouette of George Lazenby is seen in the credits of *OHMSS* and Roger Moore appears in the credits of *The Spy Who Loved Me*, *Moonraker*, *For Your Eyes Only*, *Octopussy* and *A View To A Kill*.

Also in the credits sequence of *Goldfinger* is a brief Q-branch scene, but this does not appear later on in the film. It shows Bond walking along with a Royal Mail van behind him. There are also brief glimpses of a scene from the previous film, *From Russia With Love*.

CRITICS CORNER: Here follows a selection of quotes from newspaper and magazine critics about Bond and the 007 series:

'Bond should not be allowed to survive. He is a sadist and a rapist.' *Pravda Editorial, 1965.*

'A dazzling object lesson in the principle that nothing succeeds like excess.' *Penelope Gilliat on Goldfinger.*

'The screenplay stands on tiptoe at the outermost edge of the suggestive and gazes yearningly down into the obscene.' *John Simon on Thunderball.*

'A nice balance between fantasy and realism, humour and excitement.' *the Daily Express review of The Spy Who Loved Me.*

'Bags of zest... one of Roger Moore's best.' *Octopussy reviewed by Betty Jennings in Photoplay.*

'What more could Bond fans want?' *The Guardian on A View To A Kill.*

CZECH OUT: United Artists signed Czech actor Jan Werich to portray Ernst Stavro Blofeld in *You Only Live Twice*. But the actor fell ill before shooting and had to be replaced. The last-minute replacement was British actor Donald Pleasence, complete with sinister eye make-up.

BIBI DAHL: The young protégé of Kristatos, played by Lynn-Holly Johnson. Bibi is an extremely talented eighteen-year-old ice-skater who, when she meets Bond during the course of *For Your Eyes Only*, is training hard to win the gold medal at the next Olympic Games. Bibi is something of a Lolita and much humour is derived during the movie from her attempts to bed James Bond who, rather gentlemanly, decides she is a little too young for him. Bibi eventually becomes disenchanted with Kristatos (Julian Glover) when she discovers his true nature and the film ends with her having discovered a new mentor – Kristatos' arch-rival, Columbo (Topol).

Lynn-Holly Johnson, herself a top-class ice-skater, has been a successful model and actress. She proved very popular with audiences as Bibi. Miss Johnson revealed during the filming of *For Your Eyes Only* that she had only ever seen one James Bond film – the previous one in the series, *Moonraker*.

TIMOTHY DALTON: Shakespearian actor Timothy Dalton was announced as the fourth screen 007 on August 6, 1986. This followed Roger Moore's retirement from the world of Bond after making *A View To A Kill*. Dalton's selection as 007 ended almost six months of intense media speculation.

Dalton has appeared in the critically acclaimed films *The Lion In Winter* and *Mary Queen Of Scots*. In contrast he has also worked with *Dynasty* star Joan Collins in the television mini-series, *Sins*. His 007 début is in *The Living Daylights*, filmed in Austria, Morocco and Gibraltar.

DELTA 9: A nerve gas used in *Goldfinger* is Delta 9. During his lecture on Operation Grand Slam – the code word for the assault on Fort Knox – *Goldfinger* (Gert Frobe) explains that the gas is harmless and merely induces a state of unconsciousness for twenty-four hours.

Delta 9 is anything but harmless, however, as Goldfinger well knows and as Bond points out. By spraying it into the atmosphere around Fort Knox, Goldfinger will be killing 60,000 people. Goldfinger is indifferent and merely shrugs his shoulders, saying: 'American motorists kill that many every two years.'

PROFESSOR DENT: The first villainous scientist to feature in the series is Professor Dent (Anthony Dawson) in *Dr No*. This Jamaica-based metallurgist is in the employ of *Dr No* (Joseph Wiseman). Dent lies to 007 about the source of radioactive rock samples. Dent attempts to kill Bond but this fails and 007 returns the compliment to end Dent's activities.

MAJOR FRANÇOIS DERVAL: A NATO observer of the fatal Vulcan flight in *Thunderball*, and brother of Emilio Largo's (Adolfo Celi) mistress Domino (Claudine Auger), Major Derval (Paul Stassino) unwittingly falls for SPECTRE executioner Fiona (Luciana Paluzzi). This infatuation leads to his death when SPECTRE-created double agent Angelo sprays him with gamma gas.

Domino learns towards the end of the film that Largo was instrumental in having Derval killed and this persuades her to work with Bond.

DI-NAMIC: *For Your Eyes Only* was premiered in London on Wednesday, June 24, 1981 at the Odeon, Leicester Square. The event was attended by Prince Charles and the then Lady Diana Spencer, five weeks before the Royal wedding.

DING-DONG: Elderly pupil at the Bleeker Flying School in New Orleans, Mrs Bell (Ruth Kempf) is given a flying lesson she'll never forget in a spectacular scene from *Live And Let Die*. Mrs Bell's plane – a Cessna – is commandeered by Bond when being chased by gangsters in the employ of Mr Big (Yaphet Kotto).

Unable to take off, Bond whips around other parked aircraft in the Cessna to avoid the gangsters' cars and literally clips the Cessna's wings when ploughing through half-closed hangar doors.

Ten aircraft were prepared for destruction by the film crew for this scene. For Ruth Kempf it was her first major movie role.

DIRECTORS: The fifteen Eon-produced films have been directed by five people, all but one of whom have had more than one shot at a Bond film. Terence Young directed *Dr No*, *From Russia With Love* and *Thunderball*. Guy Hamilton directed *Goldfinger*, *Diamonds Are Forever*, *Live And Let Die* and *The Man With The Golden Gun*.

Lewis Gilbert directed *You Only Live Twice*, *The Spy Who Loved Me* and *Moonraker*. Peter Hunt directed *OHMSS* and John Glen directed *For Your Eyes Only*, *Octopussy*, *A View To A Kill* and *The Living Daylights*.

Peter Hunt and John Glen made their directorial debuts on Bond films – Hunt with *OHMSS* and Glen with *For Your Eyes Only*. Both served on earlier Bond productions in the capacity of editor and second unit director.

DISCO VOLANTE: A sleek yacht, the Disco Volante, is an integral part of Emilio Largo's (Adolfo Celi) operation in *Thunderball* to steal two atomic bombs from the NATO powers. Ostensibly a millionaire's pleasure craft, the Disco Volante is in effect a floating arsenal, fitted with heavy guns and possessing an underwater hatchway to enable SPECTRE frogmen to enter and leave without being seen.

Emilio Largo is pleased with his craft and cannot help boasting to Bond of its prowess. But this astonishing craft's most spectacular asset is its ability to shed its outer cocoon and change into a speedy hydrofoil. This happens when, chased by the US Navy, Largo leaves the outer section behind to fight a rear-guard battle while he escapes with the second atomic bomb. The Disco Volante is registered in Panama.

DOLLAR DECISION: American actor John Gavin was said to have signed a contract to play 007 in *Diamonds Are Forever*.

But Sean Connery agreed to slip his shoulder holster on for the 'last time' for a sum rumoured to be in the region of a million dollars, and Gavin never made it to the first take.

DR NO: Cold, precise and unflappable – that's Dr No (Joseph Wiseman). This first Bondian screen villain is disabled. He is forced to make do with hands made of metal after an accident involving nuclear power. In his simple, white suit, Dr No is the epitome of scientific evil.

Legend has it that the scriptwriters on the early drafts for the film *Dr No* found the character as described in the Fleming novel unintentionally funny. It was suggested that the name Dr No should be given to the principle villain's pet monkey. Noël Coward, a close neighbour of Fleming in Jamaica, was offered the role of Dr No on Fleming's recommendation. But Coward's cabled reply stated: 'The answer to Dr No is No, No, No, No.'

The character is the unwanted child of a German missionary and a Chinese girl of good family. Dr No was once the treasurer of a powerful criminal organisation in China, the Tongs. He financed his radioactive complex at Crab Key in the Caribbean by escaping to America with ten million dollars of the Tongs' gold.

As a scientist, his work has afforded him a unique understanding of radioactivity. Dr No is a member of SPECTRE. The Crab Key operation, interfering with the guided instructions for US missiles, is motivated by desire for revenge on those who rejected his offer of scientific services.

Dr No dies in a battle with Bond at the climax of the picture. He slides into the boiling water which surrounds his 'critical' nuclear reactor.

DOMINO: Mistress of SPECTRE number two Emilio Largo (Adolfo Celi) and sister of the NATO pilot François Derval (Paul Stassino) is Domino (Claudine Auger), the female lead in *Thunderball*. Domino, a wild, wilful girl, is recognised by Bond because of two moles on the left thigh and a bracelet on the ankle. 007 saves Domino from drowning on their initial meeting. She is an athletic girl; an accomplished underwater swimmer with a taste for the good things in life, including caviar and champagne. She also smokes.

Despite the expensive lifestyle to which she is accustomed as the lover of Largo, whom she met in Capri, Domino readily admits to being bored with life. This is apparent in the casino sequences when she takes silent delight in Bond's whitewash of Largo at *chemin de fer*.

Domino kills Largo after discovering that the SPECTRE number two is largely responsible for her brother's death. Largo is slain during the climactic battle on board the out-of-control Disco Volante. Domino kills her lover with a harpoon gun.

'007 THEME': An exciting, pulsating piece of music, the 007 Theme was composed by John Barry for the second film in the series, *From Russia With Love*. Such was its popularity that it has been used in later movies, thus providing a degree of musical continuity throughout the series.

Distinct from the familiar James Bond Theme, which appeared in *Dr No* and has cropped up in one form or another in every film since, the '007 Theme' is featured twice in *From Russia With Love*. The composition first appears during the gunfight at the gypsy encampment and later crops up while Bond is stealing the Lektor decoder from the Russian Embassy in Istanbul.

The '007 Theme' features during the underwater battle in *Thunderball*, while Little Nellie battles it out in the skies in *You Only Live Twice*, as a background to the helicopter attack on the oil rig in *Diamonds Are Forever* and accompanies the speedboat chase in *Moonraker*.

DOUBLE TROUBLE: Occasionally in the series an actor has been required to double up for a dual role. Connery was the first to do this in *From Russia With Love*. He portrays

Bond and a SPECTRE agent created to look like 007. Actor Paul Stassino plays Major François Derval, a NATO observer, and Angelo, a SPECTRE-created double in *Thunderball*.

Charles Gray has three roles in *Diamonds Are Forever*. Gray is arch-enemy Blofeld and also takes the character of two 'Blofelds' created with the use of plastic surgery to confuse the British Secret Service. *The Man With The Golden Gun* sees 007's adversary, Scaramanga (Christopher Lee), keep a wax likeness of Bond at his fun house. Moore is called upon to play this creature.

In *Live And Let Die*, Yaphet Kotto plays Dr Kananga, the Prime Minister of San Monique, and drugs distributor Mr Big.

DRAG ACT: The keel-hauling sequence in *For Your Eyes Only* when Bond and Melina Havelock (Carole Bouquet) are tied together and pulled behind Kristatos' (Julian Glover) motor yacht is of some note in that it was the fate originally suffered by Bond and Solitaire in Ian Fleming's second novel, *Live and Let Die*. Mr Big was doing the pulling on this occasion. The sequence was not used in the film of *Live And Let Die*.

HUGO DRAX: Played by French actor Michael Lonsdale, Hugo Drax is the billionaire villain in *Moonraker*. He is a man with a horrific vision – to destroy the human race and repopulate the world with perfect physical specimens conceived aboard an orbiting space station.

Everything about Drax is larger than life. His home is an immense estate in California which accommodates his residence, a French château moved stone-by-stone to the US, and the main complex where Drax Industries assemble the Moonraker space shuttle for the US Government. Drax's personal pilot, Corinne Dufour (Corinne Clery), tells Bond, in jest, that Drax once bought the Eiffel Tower but the French Government refused him an export permit.

Drax is a cultivated man. He plays the piano, quotes Oscar Wilde and enjoys afternoon tea which he considers England's 'one, indisputable, contribution to Western civilisation.' His choice of pets is bizarre. He has two Dobermann dogs, vicious enough to devour erring employees – a fate suffered by Miss Dufour. Drax also has a python snake to which he attempts to offer 007 as a meal.

But above all else, Drax is a man of space. His vision is immense. A space station shielded from earth by means of a radar jamming system is typical, an entire city among the stars.

Drax is killed by Bond aboard the space station when Drax's finely wrought dream is thwarted by an attack of US Space Marines aboard an American military shuttle.

DRAX AIR FREIGHT: Operating out of San Pietro Airport near Rio De Janeiro is Drax Air Freight, a subsidiary of the Drax Group featured in *Moonraker*. Head of the firm is Hugo Drax (Michael Lonsdale), 007's chief adversary in the film.

DRESSED FOR THE OCCASION: An essential feature of the Bondian wardrobe is the dinner jacket. In the series he rarely travels without one and, whether black or white, Bond wears a dinner jacket in eleven of the fourteen Eon-produced films. The exceptions are *From Russia With Love*, *You Only Live Twice* and *Live And Let Die*.

Bond predominantly prefers a black dinner jacket and is seen wearing one in *Dr No*, *Thunderball*, *On Her Majesty's Secret Service*, *The Spy Who Loved Me*, *Moonraker* and *For Your Eyes Only*. Bond wears an elegant white affair in *The Man With The Golden Gun*, while in four other features – *Goldfinger*, *Diamonds Are Forever*, *Octopussy* and *A View To A Kill* – he seems undecided and wears both black and white in different sequences.

DUBBING: Actors reputed to have had their voices dubbed

in the series include Daniela Bianchi (Tatiana Romanova) in *From Russia With Love*, Gert Frobe (Goldfinger) and Shirley Eaton (Jill Masterson) in *Goldfinger* and Gabriele Ferzetti (Marc Ange Draco) in *OHMSS*.

CORINNE DUFOUR: Hugo Drax's (Michael Lonsdale) personal pilot in *Moonraker*, Miss Dufour is played by French actress Corinne Clery. As engaging girl, Corinne Dufour's warm welcome to Bond upon his arrival at the Drax Estate in California is in contrast to the initial frosty response given by *Moonraker's* female lead, Holly Goodhead (Lois Chiles). Drax repays Miss Dufour's dalliance with 007 by allowing his savage Dobermann Pinscher dogs to track her down and kill her. Thus, according to Drax, 'terminating' her employment.

FAYE DUNAWAY: Film star Faye Dunaway has twice been linked with leading female roles in Bond films. In 1965 it was claimed that Broccoli had negotiated with her agent for her to take the role of Domino in *Thunderball*. The part was eventually played by Claudine Auger. In 1982 it was strongly rumoured that Miss Dunaway would take the title role of *Octopussy*, but the character was played in the feature by Maud Adams.

'ELLO, 'ELLO, 'ELLO: Bond occasionally falls foul of the police on his secret service assignments. Bond is pursued by American police officers in three films: *Diamonds Are Forever*, *Live And Let Die* and *A View To A Kill*. Perhaps the most memorable clash with the law is in *Live And Let Die*. Sheriff J. W. Pepper (Clifton James) of the Louisiana police department does his best to hamper Bond's activities in a well-staged boat chase.

Bond's pursuit of Scaramanga (Christopher Lee) is a highlight of *The Man With The Golden Gun* and this leads to a car chase involving the Thai traffic police. In a tense race against time in *Octopussy*, Bond talks to a stolen car as he attempts to thwart the detonation of a nuclear device. He is pursued by two cars and a motorcyclist of the West German police. In *A View To A Kill*, Bond and Stacey Sutton (Tanya Roberts) are chased through the night-time streets of San Francisco in a stolen fire engine by the city's police force.

EMPIRE CHEMICALS: Bond, posing as the mysterious Mr Fisher, claims to be the managing director of Empire Chemicals when he infiltrates Osato Chemicals and Engineering of Tokyo during his mission in *You Only Live Twice*. Head of Osato Chemicals and Engineering is Mr Osato (Teru Shimada), also a SPECTRE agent. He asks Bond what happened to Williamson, the previous managing director of Empire Chemicals. 007 replies that Williamson fell into a pulveriser at the works.

EON PRODUCTIONS: The Eon Productions film company which makes the Bond series was formed by a partnership between Cubby Broccoli and Harry Saltzman in 1961. The company was created principally to bring 007 to the cinema screen. The partnership lasted until 1975 when Saltzman sold his interest in Bond to United Artists. Broccoli began producing the series on his own, starting with *The Spy Who Loved Me* in 1977.

It was occasionally an uneasy alliance between the two and both were involved in other areas of film-making during their time together. Broccoli made *Chitty Chitty Bang Bang* in 1968, while Saltzman made several films, including the Harry Palmer spy series and blockbuster Battle of Britain in 1969.

BILL FAIRBANKS: British agent Bill Fairbanks, formerly 002, is mentioned but not seen in *The Man With The Golden Gun*. Fairbanks is a victim of the assassin Scaramanga (Christopher Lee). He was shot with one of Scaramanga's golden bullets while in Beirut in 1969. Fairbanks was relaxing with a cabaret dancer Saida at the time.

FAMOUS FIVE: Five major cities have been direct targets of villains in the series, four of which are in the United States. Miami, Florida is the target for SPECTRE's atomic devices in *Thunderball*. In *Diamonds Are Forever*, Ernst Stavro Blofeld (Charles Gray) focuses the immense power of his diamond-encrusted super laser on Washington. Blofeld comes within seconds of destroying the city.

New York and Moscow are the simultaneous targets of Karl Stromberg's (Curt Jurgens) stolen nuclear missiles in *The Spy Who Loved Me*. Stromberg hopes the destruction of the cities will precipitate a global nuclear war. Max Zorin (Christopher Walken) attempts to corner the world monopoly in micro-chip production in *A View To A Kill* as part of his plan to destroy the Silicon Valley area south of San Francisco. Zorin engineers a plan to cause the San Andreas fault to move in such a way that the valley would be flooded.

JIM FANNING: Secret service art expert Jim Fanning (Douglas Wilmer) appears in *Octopussy*. He accompanies Bond to Sotherby's for the auction of a rare Fabergé egg. 007 hopes to get a lead on a jewellery smuggling caper and solves the death of 009 (Andy Bradford) in the process.

PATRICIA FEARING: A nurse at the Shrublands Health Clinic where Bond is sent to recuperate, presumably resting from the injuries suffered in the pre-credits sequence in *Thunderball*, is Patricia Fearing (Molly Peters). She saves Bond's life after the traction machine he is strapped to is sabotaged by SPECTRE agents Count Lippe (Guy Doleman). Miss Fearing is seduced twice by 007, once in the steam cabinet and later in his room.

FELDSTADT AIRFORCE BASE: Target of General Orlov's (Steven Berkoff) terrorist outrage in *Octopussy* is Feldstadt USAF base. Orlov hopes that the detonation of a Soviet nuclear bomb at the base will dupe the world into thinking that an American bomb has been triggered off accidentally. He hopes that this will force NATO powers to abandon nuclear weapons. This will leave, according to Bond, 'every border undefended for you (the Russians) to walk across at will'.

FIGURE IT OUT: There is a continuity error in *Dr No* when Miss Taro (Zena Marshall), a female agent of Dr No (Joseph Wiseman), gives Bond her address as 239, Magenta Drive. Yet later when Bond ordered a taxi to her home he gives the number as 2171.

FILLET OF SOUL: The Fillet of Soul chain of restaurants and bars across the United States features in *Live And Let Die*. It is owned by Mr Big (Yaphet Kotto). The business is used to distribute Mr Big's heroin – two tons with a street value well in excess of one billion dollars. 007 visits two Fillet of Soul restaurants; one in New York where he first encounters Mr Big and the other in New Orleans where two agents, Hamilton (Bob Dix) and Harold Strutter (Lon Satton), have been murdered by agents of Mr Big.

FINAL FLINGS: A mid-series trait is that of the surviving villainous henchman making a last-ditch attack on Bond and the leading lady after the demise of the original villain. This device presumably is a means of providing the audience with a last unexpected thrill before they leave their seats.

Mr Wint and Mr Kidd (Bruce Glover and Putter Smith) begin this in splendid style at the conclusion of *Diamonds Are Forever*. Disguised as waiters, they serve 007 and Tiffany Case (Jill St John) with an 'explosive meal' aboard the Canberra. A confusion over wine – Mr Wint displays an ignorance of Mouton Rothschild '55 – exposes the murderous pair. Bond despatches them to early graves.

Tee Hee (Julius W. Harris), one-armed henchman of Mr Big (Yaphet Kotto) in *Live And Let Die*, attacks Bond and Solitaire (Jane Seymour) on board the night train ferrying them from New Orleans to New York, while diminutive manservant Nick Nack (Herve Villechaize) attacks Bond and Mary Goodnight (Britt Ekland) with a knife in a closing scene in *The Man With The Golden Gun*. This occurs aboard Scaramanga's (Christopher Lee) Chinese junk.

The latest example of this trait happens in *The Spy Who Loved Me*. Jaws (Richard Kiel) tackles Bond in Atlantis after 007's shooting of Karl Stromberg (Curt Jurgens). *Diamonds Are Forever*, *Live And Let Die* and *The Man With The Golden Gun* were directed by Guy Hamilton.

FINGER TRAP: A deviously clever device – perhaps the nastiest in the series used by Bond – is the finger trap employed by 007 in the pre-credits sequence of *Diamonds Are Forever*. A guard working for Blofeld (Charles Gray) reaches into Bond's jacket to remove the Walther PPK and finds his fingers crushed in a trap.

FIRE POWER: Fire extinguishers have been used twice by Bond to disable opponents during an action scene. In *Diamonds Are Forever*, during the fight with Peter Franks (Joe Robinson) outside Tiffany Case's (Jill St John) apartment, 007 temporarily blinds Franks by spraying the contents of the extinguisher into his opponent's face. Bond then swings the empty container round and Franks falls to his death over the balcony.

Bond and Holly Goodhead (Lois Chiles) in *Moonraker* are cornered in the back of a speeding ambulance. 007 kicks a small fire extinguisher into action to distract the attention of his captor. This gives 007 enough time to deal with the villain.

FIRST DEGREE: We are told in *You Only Live Twice* that Bond gained a first in Oriental languages at Cambridge University.

FIRST FIGHT: *Dr No* sees Bond involved in his first fight. This follows the car chase on the way from Kingston Airport, Jamaica. 007 tackles an agent of Dr No, a 'Mr

Jones', a driver sent from Government House. Bond's defeated opponent kills himself by means of a cyanide capsule in a cigarette.

FISHY GOINGS-ON: Bond villains are keen on fish. Dr No (Joseph Wiseman) has a home with views of the ocean bed through ten-feet thick glass panels. Blofeld in *From Russia With Love* keeps a tank of Siamese fighting fish in his quarters aboard the SPECTRE yacht.

In *Thunderball*, Emilio Largo (Adolfo Celi) has a swimming pool containing sharks. Blofeld (Donald Pleasence) returns in *You Only Live Twice* with a poolfull of piranha fish at his private quarters. Mr Big (Yaphet Kotto) in *Live And Let Die* entices sharks from the ocean into his drug smuggling grotto. Karl Stromberg (Curt Jurgens) in *The Spy Who Loved Me* also keeps dangerous fish.

FLARE FOR ACTION: Three times during the series, flare pistols come to the aid of Bond. Pursued by SPECTRE speedboats near Venice in *From Russia With Love*, Bond drops several oil-drums punctured by machine gun fire into the sea. He fires a flare at the resulting oil spillage and ignites the sea, destroying the SPECTRE flotilla in a ball of flame.

In *Thunderball*, Bond is trapped in a cave by SPECTRE frogmen. He signals his whereabouts to Felix Leiter (Rik Van Nutter) in a helicopter by firing a flare through a gap in the roof of the cave.

During the pre-credits sequence in *A View To A Kill*, Bond downs a Soviet helicopter in Siberia by firing a pistol into the cabin. The resulting smoke and confusion blinds the pilot who flies into the side of a mountain leaving Bond to escape to Alsaka in a launch disguised as an ice flow.

FLASHBACKS: Thankfully, flashbacks, cumbersome devices used by film-makers to depict events that have happened earlier in the narrative, are used sparingly in the Bond series and then only briefly.

In *OHMSS*, in the scene after Tracy (Diana Rigg) has been knocked senseless by an avalanche, 007 is caught looking pensively out of the window in 'M''s office. The scene of Tracy being dragged away is relived on the window panes around Bond's face – suggesting he has only the rescue of Tracy on his mind.

Moonraker sees Bond trapped on the centrifuge trainer at Hugo Drax's (Michael Lonsdale) space centre. 007 remembers his wrist gun – capable of stopping the trainer – which 'Q' (Desmond Llewelyn) issued him in an earlier film. Brief glimpses of an earlier office scene with 'Q' are shown.

Sequences from previous Bond epics appearing in later films occur in Maurice Binder's credits for *OHMSS*. Thirteen brief glimpses of scenes from the first five films are shown. *Goldfinger* also heralds a flashback. In the credits, designed by Robert Brownjohn, the helicopter sequence from *From Russia With Love* is projected on to the gold-covered body of a model.

FLASHPOINT: One of the series' most violent scenes happens in *Dr No*. Photographer (Marguerite Lewars) is suspected by Bond of being a Dr No agent. While sitting at a table in a nightclub she smashes a light bulb into the face of Quarrel (John Kitzmiller) who hardly flinches.

FLYING CAR: A fanciful piece of equipment belonging to Scaramanga (Christopher Lee) in *The Man With The Golden Gun* is a flying car. With wings and a jet engine clipped on to the body of a vehicle, Scaramanga is able to escape the attentions of the chasing 007. When told of the car, 'M' is incredulous, but 'Q' assures him that the notion is feasible and admits that Q-branch has been working on a similar model.

FOILED AGAIN: Bond is involved in a sword fight only

twice in the series. During the climactic sequence of *Live And Let Die*, he briefly clashes blades with Baron Samedi (Geoffrey Holder) before tossing the Baron into a coffin of snakes. *Moonraker* sees 007 tackle Hugo Drax's (Michael Lonsdale) henchman, Chang (Toshiro Sugo), in Venice with a glass-handled sword borrowed from its display in a glass museum.

FORD ON BOND: Millionaire car firm boss Henry Ford II is an admirer of James Bond. He says of the character: 'Bond does a fine job demolishing many, many cars and some of them are ours.'

FORMAL OCCASION: In *Live And Let Die*, Bond addresses 'M''s (Bernard Lee) personal assistant Miss Moneypenny (Lois Maxwell) as Miss Moneypenny throughout their scenes together. This is the only time that Bond addresses his colleague in such a formal manner. In the other films of the series he simply calls her Moneypenny.

FORT KNOX: Goldfinger's raid on Fort Knox takes place on a Sunday. Goldfinger (Gert Frobe) reminds the incredulous gangsters that there are 41,000 men guarding the complex. Scriptwriters Richard Maibaum and Paul Dehn, far from covering up implausible details, have drawn attention to them. Bond tells Goldfinger that he is disappointed with Operation Grand Slam – the code name for the raid – and states it will not work.

Bond calculates that fifteen billion dollars in gold bullion to be found in Fort Knox at the time would weigh 10,500 tons and that it would take sixty men twelve days to load it into two hundred trucks. But it is then that Goldfinger reveals his devious plan to plant an atomic device and render the gold radioactive for fifty-eight years.

The combination to the safe door at Fort Knox is 36104. The atom bomb, supplied by Red China and to which Bond is handcuffed, begins its countdown at 351.

During the assault on Fort Knox an on-set in-joke creeps into the script. On the side of the military station a sign reads, 'Welcome, General Russhon'. Colonel Charles Russhon was a technical adviser to Eon Productions during the making of *Goldfinger*.

PETER FRANKS: British smuggler Peter Franks (Joe Robinson) is a part of the diamond smuggling pipeline in *Diamonds Are Forever*. He is employed by Blofeld (Charles Gray) to ferry 50,000 carats of diamonds from Amsterdam to Los Angeles. But Franks is arrested at Dover before leaving for Amsterdam and 007 assumes the smuggler's identity. Franks is later killed by Bond after escaping from custody in Britain. His appearance in the Dutch capital threatens 007's mission.

FROZEN ASSET: 007's speedy means of escape from Soviet pursuers in Siberia during the pre-credits sequence of *A View To A Kill* is a well-equipped motor launch disguised as an ice floe. The vehicle is piloted by secret agent Kimberley Jones (Mary Stavin).

Miss Stavin is a former winner of the Miss World contest.

FUNERAL FACT: Hearses appear in three Bond films – twice used as a means of attack on 007. The killers of Strangways and his secretary in *Dr No* use a hearse as a getaway vehicle. Later the same hearse is used in an attempt to force 007 off a mountain road.

Travelling to the United States accompanying the body of Peter Franks (Joe Robinson), Bond in *Diamonds Are Forever* is met at Los Angeles Airport by three gangsters in a hearse. The vehicle belongs to Morton Slumber (David Bauer), the next link in the diamond-smuggling chain. There is a funeral procession scene in *Live and Let Die*.

Bond is attacked as he journeys along the canals of Venice in *Moonraker*. His assailant rises from a coffin on board a boat to hurl a knife at 007. Bond returns the compliment – killing the man who falls conveniently back into the coffin.

PUSSY GALORE: Honor Blackman, best known for her stylish appearances in early series of the television adventure, *The Avengers*, plays Pussy Galore, a tough test pilot employed by Auric Goldfinger (Gert Frobe). Pussy is skilled in judo and no shrinking violet. We see her at the controls of Goldfinger's Lockheed Jetstar, a USAF private jet and a helicopter. Pussy is in charge of a team of female pilots, appropriately named Pussy Galore's Flying Circus.

Miss Galore's share of the proceeds from Operation Grand Slam is set to make her a rich woman. She intends to buy and settle down on a small island. Pussy rejects overtures from Goldfinger and at first is seemingly impervious to the charms of 007 but a roll in the hay with Bond at Auric Stud seems to change her mind.

Like *Octopussy* nearly twenty years later, Pussy Galore's name caused concern with the producers who felt that an eager censor might object to the sexual overtones. But the solution came when Honor Blackman was photographed with Prince Phillip at a charity dance. The *Daily Express* ran the story and picture under the headline, 'Pussy and the Prince'. The Prince did not object and neither did the censor.

An interesting footnote is that Miss Blackman's late brother, Steve Black, was in the same unit in the Army as Roger Moore.

GAMBLING: Casinos and forms of gambling have been a feature of the series. The first scene in which 007 appears – at the Le Cercle Club in *Dr No* – sees 007 and Sylvia Trench (Eunice Gayson) battling it out across the card table in a game of *chemin de fer*.

In *Thunderball*, SPECTRE's number two, Emilio Largo (Adolfo Celi), first comes across 007 in a Nassau casino. A casino also provides the background for Bond's second meeting with his future bride, Tracy (Diana Rigg) in *OHMSS*.

Much of *Diamonds Are Forever* revolves around Las Vegas and the action often focuses on casinos in the desert city. In pursuit of Scaramanga (Christopher Lee) in *The Man With The Golden Gun*, Bond tails Lazar (Marne Maitland) – Scaramanga's golden bullet maker – to a casino in Macau. It is here 007 meets the striking Andrea (Maud Adams).

GAMMA GAS: Used in *Thunderball* by SPECTRE assassin Fiona (Luciana Paluzzi), Gamma gas, claimed to have an instantaneous effect, is shot initially from a pistol to kill Major Derval (Paul Stassino) as a prelude to SPECTRE agent Angelo's impersonation of him. Later, Angelo arms himself with a canister of Gamma gas to kill the crew of the Vulcan bomber carrying two atomic warheads. This is achieved by inserting the gas into the oxygen supply of the aircraft.

GEIGER COUNTER: The first gadget to feature in the series is a geiger counter in *Dr No*. 007 uses the device to measure radioactivity in the area near Dr No's (Joseph Wiseman) Crab Key island complex. The geiger counter is delivered to Bond in Jamaica by diplomatic pouch. It is simply wrapped in brown paper.

GEMS: Diamonds are the central theme of *Diamonds Are Forever*. A massive supply of diamonds accumulated by Blofeld (Charles Gray) is incorporated into a super laser satellite to threaten the world. Diamonds also feature in *Thunderball*. They are the ransom – £100 million in uncut gems – demanded by SPECTRE for the return of two stolen atomic bombs.

LEWIS GILBERT: A prestigious British director whose credits include *Alfie* and *Educating Rita*, Lewis Gilbert has directed three Bond films: *You Only Live Twice*, *The Spy Who Loved Me* and *Moonraker*.

If Guy Hamilton's style suited Sean Connery, then the same could be said for the combination of Lewis Gilbert and Roger Moore. Having directed Connery in *You Only Live Twice*, Gilbert returned to the series after a ten-year gap to direct *The Spy Who Loved Me*, arguably the best in the series. It was Roger Moore's third Bond picture and the one that the actor regards as his personal favourite.

Gilbert is particularly talented at presenting an epic scope to a picture and this is in evidence in the Japanese location scenes for *You Only Live Twice* and the Egyptian episodes of *The Spy Who Loved Me*.

GIRL TALK: Tula, one of the Bond girls hired for *For Your Eyes Only*, was born a man in Norfolk. She underwent a sex-change operation six years before her part in the Bond film. Tula's secret was revealed by Mayfair magazine several weeks after the film's première.

GLAMOUR GIRLS: Goldfinger introduces Bond fans to Pussy Galore's (Honor Blackman) Flying Circus. The circus consists of five female pilots flying Cherokee Piper light aircraft. This high-flying team is an essential part of Goldfinger's (Gert Frobe) audacious assault on Fort Knox.

JOHN GLEN: For most 007 fans, John Glen is the quintessential Bondian director. His direction of *For Your Eyes Only*, *Octopussy*, *A View To A Kill* and *The Living Daylights* combines perfectly the elements of gritty, realistic excitement and the familiar 007 fantasy machine.

Glen began in the film business in 1947. Among the films he has worked on are classics like *The Third Man* and *The Wooden Horse*. Turning to television he edited the *Danger Man* series and also gained experience of second unit directing.

His directoral debut was with *For Your Eyes Only* in 1981, but he was no stranger to the 007 stage having served as editor and second unit director on *OHMSS*, *The Spy Who*

Loved Me and *Moonraker*.

He once said of James Bond: 'He's very British and he has this tremendous flair for being gallant. There is a formula to these films, though it's very difficult to define. Cubby Broccoli is the expert that makes a Bond film tick, but, basically, it is a combination of many things. There's an honesty to the way we make these movies – we don't cheat the public.'

Glen's particular strength is his handling of action sequences, a trait he shares with Peter Hunt, another editor-turned-director; Glen always manages to bring a new angle to any chase. He is also the only director to helm four consecutive 007 adventures.

GLEN ON BOND: 'Pre-planning is very important in a Bond film because the nature of the beast is that you have to delegate an awful lot to second unit directors.' *Director John Glen, reflecting on the job in 1981.*

GLOBAL POLITICS: Bond films over the years have provided a fascinating parallel to what's happening across the world in respect of East-West relations. The films have mirrored the twists and turns of global politics but have never attempted to influence or judge. In the early 1960s the Cold War was beginning to thaw and East-West relations were improving in the wake of the Cuban missile crisis.

Cubby Broccoli and Harry Saltzman moved away from Fleming's concept of having the Soviet Union as the principal villain and provided other backers for the bad guys. Thus 1963's *From Russia With Love* featured a SPECTRE conspiracy as opposed to the purely Soviet enterprise of the novel. Goldfinger (Gert Frobe) is a freelance villain backed by Red China in the 1964 film of the same name. The literary character was treasurer of SMERSH.

In 1967's *You Only Live Twice*, Blofeld's SPECTRE is once again backed by Red China – at least we are supposed to believe it is Red China, although the film never specifies. At that time during the 1960s the West was concerned at the activities of the hard-line Chairman Mao in China.

Moving on to the 1970s and the period of the détente, we find that Scaramanga (Christopher Lee), the principal villain of *The Man With The Golden Gun* (1974), was trained by the KGB but he is now a freelance killer working for China.

The Spy Who Loved Me (1977) sees Bond and the Soviet Union working side by side. Bond is set to be killed by a Russian hit-squad in the pre-credits sequence but the film is barely a third over before the British and the Soviets have joined forces to investigate the theft of nuclear submarines by Karl Stromberg (Curt Jurgens).

Contrary to popular belief, the Soviet Union is not seen as Bond's main foe until *For Your Eyes Only* (1981) and even then the Soviets act only as backers for Kristatos (Julian Glover) as he attempts to salvage the sunken British spy ship, the St George's.

Only in *Octopussy* (1983) – as the Cold War begins to bite again – do we find a Russian villain, General Orlov (Steven Berkoff) and he is a renegade, disowned by his own secret service when he attempts to blow up a USAF base in West Germany.

Max Zorin (Christopher Walken) has been a Soviet agent in the past – the KGB trained him – but he announces half-way through *A View To A Kill* (1985) that he has become an independent in order to concentrate on his plans to destroy Silicon Valley.

GOBINDA: Indian tough guy in *Octopussy*, Gobinda (Kabir Bedi) is Kamal Khan's (Louis Jourdan) right-hand man and bodyguard. Gobinda meets his death during the exciting aeroplane sequence just before the end of the film when Bond resorts to his very own version of aerial combat.

GENERAL GOGOL: The KGB equivalent of 'M', General

Gogol, is first introduced in *The Spy Who Loved Me*. He has since become a regular character in the series, making appearances in *Moonraker*, *For Your Eyes Only*, *Octopussy*, *A View To A Kill* and *The Living Daylights*. Played by Walter Gotell, Gogol's role has ranged from the important to the cameo. Values and attitudes to the character also differ. In *The Spy Who Loved Me*, Gogol and his department are allies of the British and fighting the common enemy of Karl Stromberg (Curt Jurgens). But in *For Your Eyes Only*, while not the true villain, he is supporting Kristatos' (Julian Glover) quest for the lost British ATAC transmitter.

Gogol and 'M' have a high regard for each other. *The Spy Who Loved Me* reveals that they are on first name terms and at the conclusion of *Octopussy* and *A View To A Kill*, Gogol is allowed the privilege of enjoying a drink at the home of the British Secret Service, 'M''s office. General Gogol is allowed one minor weakness – besides a liking for alcohol – a suggested affair with his secretary, Rublevitch (Eva Rueber-Staier).

Walter Gotell also played the SPECTRE trainer Morzeny in *From Russia With Love*.

GOLDEN TOUCH: The death of Jill Masterson (Shirley Eaton) – painted from head to toe in gold so that she dies from skin suffocation – in *Goldfinger* sets a precedent for the series. Women who appear in the early sequences of Bond pictures, especially those who have formed some romantic attachment, are often killed off swiftly.

Other unfortunates include: Paula (Martine Beswick) and Fiona (Luciana Paluzzi) in *Thunderball*; Aki (Akiko Wakabayashi) in *You Only Live Twice*; Plenty O'Toole (Lana Wood) in *Diamonds Are Forever*; Rosie Carver (Gloria Hendry) in *Live And Let Die*; Andrea (Maud Adams) in *The Man With The Golden Gun*; Corrine Dufour (Corrine Clery) in *Moonraker* and Lisl (Cassandra Harris) in *For Your Eyes Only*.

AURIC GOLDFINGER: Despite having a name which, according to Bond, sounds 'like a French nail varnish', Goldfinger is the series' only major villain who hails from Britain. Played by German actor Gert Frobe, known in his own country as a comedian, Goldfinger is a mountain of a man. He is the only villian of the Connery era not to be backed by SPECTRE and the character develops as one of Eon Productions' most successful.

Like many Bondian villains, he is super rich. Goldfinger runs a string of metallurgical installations in Switzerland. This is where Bond stumbles on his method of smuggling gold. Goldfinger enjoys playing golf and drinking mint juleps. He breeds horses, but his overwhelming passion is for gold.

Goldfinger's Rolls Royce carries the personal number plate AU 1.

GOLF: Favourite pastime of Bond's creator, Ian Fleming, golf was featured in the Bond novels and has in three instances been carried over to the big screen. In *Dr No*, Bond finds that he and Sylvia Trench (Eunice Gayson) share a common interest in the sport. Later, Bond discovers the scantily clad Miss Trench in his flat. She is practising her putting technique.

Goldfinger features the memorable encounter between Bond and Goldfinger (Gert Frobe). To begin with they play 'a shilling a hole' but as the game goes on the stakes are upped. In this sequence we learn that Bond plays with a Penfold Hearts ball.

OHMSS shows George Lazenby's Bond emerging from his hotel only to be kidnapped by employees of his future father-in-law, Draco (Gabriele Ferzetti). Bond is on his way to a round of golf with his clubs slung over his shoulder.

HOLLY GOODHEAD: Arguably the most accomplished female lead in the series, Dr Holly Goodhead (Lois Chiles) appears in *Moonraker*. Holly was schooled in the top US girls' college, Vassar. She is a fully qualified NASA-trained astronaut and capable of flying a space shuttle. Holly is also a CIA agent. She is haughty, disdainful and holds 007 in less than high regard. Holly's standard CIA equipment includes a pen which contains poisoned ink, a bottle of Dior perfume which transforms into a flamethrower, a nasty dart in a diary and a concealed radio in her handbag.

MARY GOODNIGHT: British Secret Service agent Mary Goodnight (Britt Ekland), stationed in South East Asia, encounters Bond in Hong Kong in *The Man With The Golden Gun*. It appears that 007 and Mary are no strangers and know each other well, although they have not met for two years because of Goodnight's posting to the Far East. Mary drives an open-topped MG sportscar, registration number AL 8083. Her standard secret service issue formal dress includes a homing device in the bottom button.

Ekland was originally tested for the role of Andrea – eventually played by Maud Adams – the mistress of *The Man With The Golden Gun*.

DONALD GRANT: A perfect human killing machine, Grant (Robert Shaw) is one of the enduring images of the early films. The clever trick of the film-makers is that Grant is kept silent in *From Russia With Love* until the last third of the film. This maintains the suspense. Grant appears to be unemotional about his work. He shadows Bond throughout the film, making sure the British agent stays alive until he reaches SPECTRE's chosen killing ground. Indeed, during the fight at the gipsy camp, Grant saves 007's life by killing one of the Bulgarians.

Among Grant's nasty bag of tricks is a wristwatch containing a strand of wire to strangle opponents. 007 is nearly killed with this device but Bond turns the tables on Grant and strangles him with the wire.

GRAVE CONCERN: A line that haunts Bond throughout *OHMSS* is 'We have all the time in the world'. The film-makers lifted the line directly from the Fleming novel. It underlines the tragedy of Bond's meeting with Tracy, his falling in love, subsequent marriage and the death of Tracy. A song takes its title from the line. Written by John Barry and Hal David, the ballad was beautifully sung by Louis Armstrong in the film. The song appears on the soundtrack during the montage sequence showing Bond and Tracy (Diana Rigg) falling in love. The line is also Bond's last in the film – and George Lazenby's. Bond cradles the dead Tracy in his Aston Martin on their honeymoon after she has been shot by Irma Bunt (Ilse Steppat), Blofeld's female dragon of an aide.

The line is also the inscription that Bond chose for Tracy's headstone at her grave. We discover this later on in the series in a scene from *For Your Eyes Only*.

GREAT SCOT: There is only one attempt by the film-makers to make a play on Bond's Scottish ancestry. This is in *OHMSS* when 007 disguises himself as Sir Hilary Bray. Dining with Irma Bunt (Ilse Steppat) and twelve gorgeous female patients of the Piz Gloria clinic, Bond wears full Scottish regalia. Later, when seducing Ruby Bartlett (Angela Scoular), he reveals that like every true Scot he wears nothing under his kilt.

GUN LAW: Title designer Maurice Binder's familiar gun barrel sequence first appears in *Dr No*, but it is accompanied by unusual sound effects as opposed to an arrangement of the James Bond Theme which accompanies it in later films. Binder came up with the idea in fifteen minutes.

'Even though I didn't know what *Dr No* was all about, I was becoming involved in another project, so I had to do *Dr No* in a hurry. And I had to design a title to show just what I wanted to do,' he once explained. *Dr No* is unique in that there is no pre-credits sequence.

'I figured the gunshot thing across the screen would be effective. I had these little white stickers and I put them on a black storyboard. I thought it would be a good idea to look down the barrel and see James Bond as he walked out ... firing at you. And then the blood comes down the screen. As we know, the idea was approved.'

The title designs display Binder's penchant for circles – a fact that is evident as the series progresses.

HAMILTON: An uncredited CIA agent, Hamilton features briefly in *Diamonds Are Forever*. The character accompanies Felix Leiter (Norman Burton) and his name undoubtedly owes a lot to the director of the film, Guy Hamilton. In the following film, *Live And Let Die*, another Hamilton appears again – only to be murdered in the New Orleans pre-credits sequence – but there is doubt whether this agent, played by Bob Dix, is supposed to be the same character.

GUY HAMILTON: A highly respected British director and former assistant to Carol Reed, Guy Hamilton was hired by Eon Productions to direct the third Bond film, *Goldfinger*. Hamilton's forte is high polish, panache and lighthearted wit. His success with the phenomenally successful *Goldfinger* resulted in Eon Productions asking him to direct three other Bonds: *Diamonds Are Forever*, *Live And Let Die* and *The Man With The Golden Gun*.

Hamilton's light touch perfectly complements Sean Connery's tough image. His two Connery Bonds, *Goldfinger* and *Diamonds Are Forever* are usually regarded as the best of Connery's appearances.

With Roger Moore, whose approach to the role was lighter than Connery's, Hamilton is less successful. Although the crocodile sequences and the speedboat chase in *Live And Let Die* display a masterly touch.

HAPPY RETURNS: Many supporting actors and actresses

have made more than one appearance in the Bond series portraying a different character in each film.

Shane Rimmer is the actor who has appeared the most times. To date he has played three different parts: an unnamed role in *You Only Live Twice*; Tom, an employee of Willard Whyte (Jimmy Dean), in *Diamonds Are Forever* and Commander Carter, captain of the USS Wayne submarine, in *The Spy Who Loved Me*.

Other returns have been made by Joseph Wiseman in *Dr No* and *Thunderball*; Anthony Dawson in *Dr No* and *From Russia With Love*; Martine Beswick in *From Russia With Love* and *Thunderball*; Walter Gotell in *From Russia With Love* and regularly as General Gogol from *The Spy Who Loved Me* onwards; Charles Gray in *You Only Live Twice* and *Diamonds Are Forever*; David Bauer in *You Only Live Twice* and *Diamonds Are Forever*; Maud Adams in *The Man With The Golden Gun* and *Octopussy*; George Baker in *OHMSS* and *The Spy Who Loved Me*; Mary Stavin in *Octopussy* and *A View To A Kill*; Burt Kwouk in *Goldfinger* and *You Only Live Twice*; Nadja Regin in *From Russia With Love* and *Goldfinger*; Ed Bishop in *You Only Live Twice* and *Diamonds Are Forever*; Anthony Chin in *You Only Live Twice* and *A View To A Kill*; Robert Brown in *The Spy Who Loved Me* and 'M' in *Octopussy* and *A View To A Kill*; Kim Fortune in *The Spy Who Loved Me* and *Moonraker*; Albert Moses in *The Spy Who Loved Me* and *Octopussy*.

ADMIRAL HARGREAVES: A minor character in *The Spy Who Loved Me*, Admiral Hargreaves is worthy of note because he is played by Robert Brown who returned to the series in *Octopussy* and *A View To A Kill* as 'M'.

HAT-TRICK: The classic scenes when Bond walks into Miss Moneypenny's (Lois Maxwell) office and throws his hat on to the hat stand were never as easy as they looked. Often during shooting no one on the set could manage to do the trick – at times even producer Cubby Broccoli had a go. On some occasions it took as many as eighty throws before there was a shot good enough for the can.

MELINA HAVELOCK: The female lead in *For Your Eyes Only*, Melina Havelock (Carole Bouquet), is the half Greek, half English daughter of Sir Timothy (Jack Hedley) and Lady Iona (Toby Robins) Havelock. When her parents are murdered in an appalling manner by Hector Gonzales (Stephen Kalipha) she sets out to avenge the killing. Melina encounters James Bond en route. Bond is attempting to recover the lost ATAC transmitting device which Sir Timothy Havelock, a noted marine archaeologist and British secret agent, has been trying to locate.

Melina is young but stubborn and determined. Above all, she is highly intelligent – like her father, a marine archaeologist. Melina is also an accomplished diver and expert shot with a crossbow. It is the latter skill which saves Bond's life when he has been captured by Gonzales. Melina's expertise in marine exploration is indispensable when Bond locates the ATAC.

French actress Carole Bouquet's other work includes parts in Bertrand Blier's *Buffet Froid* and Luis Buñuel's *That Obscure Object Of Desire*.

HEAT SIGNATURE RECOGNITION: A tracking process outlined by 'Q' (Desmond Llewelyn) at the beginning of *The Spy Who Loved Me* is heat signature recognition. In short, a satellite with infra-red sensors can recognise a nuclear missile in flight by its tail fire. According to 'Q', the submarine tracking system for sale to the highest bidder – a system that threatens the entire defence strategy of the West – works on exactly the same principle, identifying a submerged submarine by its wake.

HELGA: Number eleven in the SPECTRE hierarchy, the red-haired Helga (Karin Dor) in *You Only Live Twice* is much in the same mould as *Thunderball*'s female assassin, Fiona Volpe (Luciana Paluzzi). Helga is the personal assistant to SPECTRE agent Mr Osato (Teru Shimada). But her failure to eliminate 007 leads to her death at the hands of Blofeld (Donald Pleasence). He feeds her to his pet piranha fish.

HENCHMAN: The appearance of Oddjob (Harold Sakata), silent, mute and implacable, in *Goldfinger*, is the first of what is to become a standard fixture in Bond movies – the henchman.

These characters would often steal the show from the main villain. Other memorable henchman are Mr Wint (Bruce Glover) and Mr Kidd (Putter Smith) in *Diamonds Are Forever*; Tee-hee (Julius H. Harris), he of the metal claw and maniacal laugh in *Live And Let Die*; the diminutive Nick-Nack (Herve Villechaize, who also found fame in television's *Fantasy Island*), in *The Man With The Golden Gun*; the seven-foot two-inch , steel-toothed monster, Jaws (Richard Kiel) in *The Spy Who Loved Me* who joined forces with Hugo Drax (Michael Lonsdale) in *Moonraker* (Jaws is the only henchman to return in the series); Gobinda (Kabir Bedi), Kamal Khan's Indian helper in *Octopussy* and May Day (Grace Jones), Max Zorin's (Christopher Walken) black bodyguard and lover in *A View To A Kill*.

HENDERSON: Bond's contact in Japan during the initial stages of *You Only Live Twice* is Henderson (Charles Gray). Henderson is unquestionably British but having spent twenty-eight years living in Japan he has become almost like a native of the country. His home – where he meets 007 – is a curious mixture of styles.

Henderson has a wooden leg. He lost his left leg in Singapore in 1942 during World War II. He makes the error of providing Bond with a Martini, stirred but not shaken. Perhaps out of respect for Henderson's experience and seniority, 007 assures him that it is just right and even compliments his host on using Russian vodka. Henderson murmurs that he gets his supply from the doorman at the Soviet Embassy, 'among certain other things'.

Henderson does not last long enough to be of much

practical use to Bond since he is murdered by a knife-wielding assassin of Mr Osato (Teru Shimada) who is in turn an associate of Blofeld (Donald Pleasence). Charles Gray returns in *Diamonds Are Forever* as Blofeld.

HI-FAT: Oriental industrialist and employer of Scaramanga (Christopher Lee), Hi-Fat (Richard Loo) is said to be one of the richest men in South-East Asia. Hi-Fat, head of Hi-Fat Enterprises – all of them legal as far as the British Secret Service can establish – lives in luxury in a mountainside home in Bangkok surrounded by guards. Hi-Fat employs Gibson, the missing solar energy expert. Hi-Fat Enterprises run a solar energy power station on Scaramanga's island off the coast of China.

Hi-Fat lives long enough to regret employing Scaramanga, whom we learn in *The Man With The Golden Gun* starts off as the junior partner. Hi-Fat is ruthlessly killed by Scaramanga. This allows the movie's principal villain to take control of the Hi-Fat empire.

HI-JACK HIGH-JINKS: The Moonraker space shuttle featured in the film of the same name is capable of being launched into space by rocket, to orbit the earth and return to land like any conventional aircraft. The hi-jack in mid-air over Yukon Territory, Canada, of a shuttle while en route to Britain atop a jumbo jet, leads 007 onto the trail of Hugo Drax (Michael Lonsdale). His company builds the shuttles for NASA. He needs the shuttle as part of his grand scheme, Operation Orchid.

Moonraker 5, Drax's personal shuttle, is fitted with a laser in its nose.

HIGH-FLYER: *From Russia With Love* is the first film of the series to feature a scene with a helicopter. Helicopters of all shapes and sizes abound in Bond films. *Dr No* and *The Man With The Golden Gun* are the only two Bond films in which the aircraft does not appear.

HIGH NOTES: The scores for the Bond films have produced some of the most memorable songs to emerge from the cinema over the past twenty-five years. Chief contributer is Yorkshire-born composer John Barry, a four-time Oscar winner, although he has never been nominated for an award for his work on the Bonds.

Barry arranged the James Bond Theme for *Dr No*. This work seemed to highlight the electric excitement which the movie generated in the early 1960s and the theme reached thirteen in the UK charts in 1962. Barry wrote the score for *From Russia With Love* but on this occasion the theme song was written by Lionel Bart. Barry went on to write the scores for *Goldfinger, Thunderball, You Only Live Twice, OHMSS, Diamonds Are Forever, The Man With The Golden Gun, Moonraker, Octopussy, A View To A Kill* and *The Living Daylights*.

Former Beatles' producer George Martin provided the score for *Live And Let Die*. Marvin Hamlisch did the same for *The Spy Who Loved Me* and Bill Conti contributed the score for *For Your Eyes Only*.

Some of the biggest names in the music business have recorded for Eon Productions. Matt Monro sang the theme to *From Russia With Love* and he was followed by Shirley Bassey (*Goldfinger*), Tom Jones (*Thunderball*), Nancy Sinatra (*You Only Live Twice*), Louis Armstrong (*OHMSS*), Miss Bassey (*Diamonds Are Forever*), Paul McCartney and Wings (*Live And Let Die*), Lulu (*The Man With The Golden Gun*), Carly Simon with 'Nobody Does It Better' (*The Spy Who Loved Me*), iss Bassey, for a third time (*Moonraker*), Sheena Easton (*For Your Eyes Only*), Rita Coolidge, with 'All Time High' (*Octopussy*) and Duran Duran (*A View To A Kill*).

Commercially, the most successful songs were *Goldfinger, You Only Live Twice, Live And Let Die, Nobody Does It Better, For Your Eyes Only* and *A View To A Kill*. Duran Duran's 'A View To A Kill' reached number two in the UK charts and was number one in the US charts in 1985.

HORSE SENSE: In *A View To A Kill* Max Zorin's (Christopher Walken) horse Pegasus seems to win races against all odds. Zorin ensures success by means of micro-chip implantation. This device is fitted into the horse's leg by means of surgery. The tiny implantation is programmed to control an injection of natural steroids which enable Pegasus to overcome fatigue during a race. The injection is triggered by a remote control transmitter fitted into the top of Zorin's cane.

HOT STUFF: Bond and KGB agent Pola Ivanova (Fiona Fullerton) take time out from the rigours of espionage in *A View To A Kill* to enjoy a sensual hot tub together at the Nippon Relaxation Spa, San Francisco.

HOVERCRAFTS: Perhaps surprisingly in a series that has featured every conceivable form of transport, hovercrafts have appeared only twice.

The first shot of a hovercraft is in *Diamonds Are Forever* when Bond, having assumed the identity of diamond smuggler Peter Franks (Joe Robinson), travels to his first contact in Holland by crossing the Channel from Dover by Hovercraft.

In *Moonraker*, the Q-Branch-equipped gondola which Bond uses in Venice converts into a hovercraft. The machine is used to carry Bond onto St Mark's Square away from the motor launch and gunmen who have been chasing him along the city's canals.

HOWE: Californian Department of Conservation official Howe (Daniel Benzali) is duped by Max Zorin (Christopher Walken) in *A View To A Kill* into believing that the villain's commercial operations are legitimate and are of some benefit to California. Howe tells Bond that the state welcomes men like Zorin with 'open arms'. Bond is posing as *Financial Times* reporter James Stock. But Howe's loyalty is not repaid. Zorin coldly shoots Howe with Bond's Walther PPK in a bid to implicate the agent with the killing. Zorin refers to this as 'intuitive improvisation'.

ALAN HUME: London-born cameraman Hume entered the film industry in 1942 and has worked on such films as *The Land That Time Forgot*, *Shout At The Devil* (which starred Roger Moore), *Return Of The Jedi* and *Supergirl*. Hume was director of photography on *For Your Eyes Only*, *Octopussy* and *A View To A Kill*.

PETER HUNT: Having worked for Eon Productions as an editor from *Dr No* onwards and as a second unit director on *You Only Live Twice*, Peter Hunt directed just one Bond film, *OHMSS* – the picture that introduced George Lazenby as Bond.

As befits a former editor, Hunt is an extremely fast-paced director and his action sequences in *OHMSS* are superbly staged and remain among the best in the series. His one Bond film at the helm, dispensed with a good deal of the gimmickry and turned out the Bond movie that remains the most faithful to Ian Fleming's original novel.

HYDROFOILS: High-powered hydrofoils feature in two Bond films. Emilio Largo's (Adolfo Celi) sleek yacht, the Disco Volante, in *Thunderball* transforms itself into a speedy hydrofoil by shedding the outer cocoon. This is a handy device if one needs to escape from the US Navy when a stolen nuclear device is in one's possession. In *The Man With The Golden Gun*, Bond trails Scaramanga's (Christopher Lee) mistress Andrea Anders (Maud Adams) aboard the Hong Kong-Macau hydrofoil.

IDENTIGRAPH: A device used to identify suspect Émile Léopold Locque (Michael Gothard) in *For Your Eyes Only* is the identigraph. Bond encounters Locque in Spain. The 3D identigraph, as displayed by 'Q' (Desmond Llewelyn) is in the experimental stage. It operates by producing a composite of the suspect: colour of eyes and width of mouth etc. The picture produced is matched with those in the photographic files of police forces throughout the world.

IMPULSE CONDUCTOR CIRCUIT: Protecting the detonator of the Polaris missile in *The Spy Who Loved Me* is an impulse conductor circuit. When magnetised, the circuit makes the removal of the missile's detonator more difficult. Bond finds out when attempting to do so. If the detonator touches any part of the circuit the missile will explode.

INJURIES: For such a man of action, it comes as no surprise to discover that Bond picks up his fair share of bumps and bruises. In *Dr No* he is beaten senseless by enemy agents, shot in the leg in *Thunderball*, cut on the shoulder in a fight with Jaws (Richard Kiel) in *The Spy Who Loved Me* and dragged over a coral reef resulting in nasty back injuries during a keel-hauling sequence in *For Your Eyes Only*. Bond has a scar on his lower back. This was pointed out twice in *From Russia With Love* – by Tatiana Romanova (Daniela Bianchi) and Sylvia Trench (Eunice Gayson).

Playing the character is not without its risks as both Sean Connery and Roger Moore found out. During the filming of the fight with Oddjob (Harold Sakata) in *Goldfinger*, Connery was thrown awkwardly, injuring his back, and walked off the set in protest. While on *The Spy Who Loved Me*, a sequence went wrong when a chair blown up by Karl Stromberg (Curt Jurgens) exploded before Moore left clear. The result was a sore bottom for Moore and dressings that had to be changed every day.

INTERNATIONAL BROTHERHOOD FOR STATELESS PERSONS: The IBFSP is a charitable cover used by SPECTRE in *Thunderball*. The offices of the Brotherhood are situated in Paris and mask the inner sanctum of SPECTRE. At the beginning of the film, Emilio Largo (Adolfo Celi) arrives to attend a board meeting where the plan to steal two atomic devices from the NATO powers is formulated. It is during this meeting that we learn of SPECTRE's involvement in the Great Train Robbery – for which the organisation earned £250,000.

I QUIT: Bond resigns from the secret service at the beginning of *OHMSS*. This is one of the occasions when he becomes exasperated with his work. 007 dictates his resignation to Miss Moneypenny (Lois Maxwell) and asks her to present it to 'M' (Bernard Lee), 'That monument,' Bond says. But Miss Moneypenny changes the letter to a request for two weeks' leave. This gives 007 plenty of time to pursue Blofeld (Telly Savalas). The mission was originally taken away from Bond because of a lack of leads.

POLA IVANOVA: A KGB agent of General Gogol (Walter Gotell), Pola Ivanova (Fiona Fullerton) is assigned by her chief to discover the exact nature of Max Zorin's (Christopher Walken) plot in *A View To A Kill*. In the course of the mission she runs into Bond who is similarly occupied.

Sharing a whirlpool spa bath at Nippon Spa, San Francisco, it transpires that 007 and Pola are old acquaintances.

JAMAICA: A favourite location for Ian Fleming's novels and short stories, the Caribbean island of Jamaica has featured in two Bond films. In *Dr No*, much of the action takes place on Jamaica and the picture affords us one of the last glimpses of the colonial island. In *Live And Let Die*, Jamaica is used for scenes from the island of San Monique, whose Prime Minister Dr Kananga (Yaphet Kotto) is the alter-ego of Harlem gangland boss Mr Big.

JAWS: Played by seven-foot two-inches actor Richard Kiel, Jaws is an eighteen stone one-man army kitted out with an awesome set of fearsome cobalt steel teeth. The character first appeared in *The Spy Who Loved Me*. He was such a success that he was allowed to survive the adventure and make a comeback in the next picture, *Moonraker* – the only henchman to do so.

Jaws was the brainchild of producer Cubby Broccoli and the role quickly established Richard Kiel as a cult figure, especially among children. He became so popular that the character was allowed to mellow in his second appearance. Jaws fell in love with a blonde girl – much smaller in stature – and he changed sides to help 007 in his battle against Hugo Drax (Michael Lonsdale). But there were many complaints from Bond fans that a former villain should be allowed to share the victory honours with the hero.

Jaws survived the second picture, too. However, having reformed and presumably married his true love (Blanche Ravalec), it is doubtful that he will appear a third time, but there again ...

JET PACK: Bond uses a jet pack to escape pursuing guards in the pre-credits sequence of *Thunderball*. The jet pack, far from being a prop, was being tested during the time *Thunderball* was made. The armed forces of the United States were working on the device and the Pentagon gave permission for a jet pack, along with a trained operator, to be flown across to France – the location for the sequence – for use by Eon Productions.

But the jet pack was later discarded by the Pentagon because of technical difficulties.

JUPITER 16: The name of the space capsule stolen by the SPECTRE interceptor rocket in the pre-credits sequence of *You Only Live Twice* is Jupiter 16. Jupiter 16 is manned by two astronauts, played by Norman Jones and Paul Carson. The next mission, presumably Jupiter 17, though the script does not specify, is manned by astronauts played by Bill Mitchell and George Roubicek.

JUST THE TICKET: Public transport on Dr Kananga's (Yaphet Kotto) sleepy Caribbean island of San Monique in *Live And Let Die* appears to consist entirely of an elderly double decker bus. The vehicle, a former London Transport No 19 bus, was shipped over to Jamaica by Eon Productions and resprayed a dull green. The bus starred in the hairraising sequence in which 007, escaping with Solitaire (Jane Seymour) from the clutches of Mr Big (Yaphet Kotto), transforms the vehicle into a single decker by driving it under a low bridge. In charge of the bus on set, and the driving tuition of Roger Moore, was Maurice Patchett, a London Transport bus driving instructor.

PRINCE KAMAL KHAN: A third of *Octopussy's* trio of villainous characters, Prince Kamal Khan (Louis Jourdan) is probably the most regal of Bondian bad guys. Kamal Khan is an exiled Afghan prince. He is an avid sportsman who plays polo, cricket and tennis. Kamal Khan also likes playing backgammon and is not averse to cheating with loaded dice. He enjoys hunting in the Indian jungle when the prey is British agents rather than tigers.

Kamal owns a sumptuous estate in India named Monsoon Palace and he employs the presence of a menacing bodyguard, Gobinda (Kabir Bedi). He flies a Beech 18 aircraft, and drives a Rolls Royce, registration number KAM 1. His eating habits are suitably bizarre and he likes nothing better than helping himself to the eyes of a stuffed sheep head and munching them with evident enjoyment.

The Prince is guilty of duplicity when he deceives Octopussy (Maud Adams) into smuggling a nuclear warhead into a USAF base in West Germany and he is quite prepared to allow General Orlov (Steven Berkoff) to get away with murdering thousands provided that he gets what he wants in return, the stolen art treasures of the Kremlin.

DR KANANGA: Alter-ego of principal villain Mr Big in *Live And Let Die* is Dr Kananga. Yaphet Kotto plays both characters. Dr Kananga, prime minister of San Monique, is heavily involved in heroin smuggling into the United States. American gangster Mr Big refines and distributes the drug. Bond quickly learns that the characters are the same person. Scriptwriter Tom Mankiewicz discovered the name during filming. The owner of the crocodile farm where memorable scenes from the movie were shot is Ross Kananga. Mankiewicz liked the sound of the name so much he decided to use it in the script.

KISS, KISS, BANG, BANG: In the early 1960s, Italian audiences nicknamed 007 Mr Kiss, Kiss, Bang, Bang. In response to this, composer John Barry wrote a song entitled 'Mr Kiss, Kiss, Bang, Bang' which appears on the soundtrack of the album of *Thunderball*.

KISS-KISS CLUB: The Kiss-Kiss nightclub in the Bahamas is near where Bond is shot in the leg by SPECTRE agents. He hides in the club during the Junkanoo sequences of *Thunderball*. After dressing his wound in the nightclub toilets, Bond attempts to hide on the dance floor but he is cornered by SPECTRE assassin Fiona Volpe (Luciana Paluzzi). As they dance, SPECTRE agents move to shoot 007 but the ever-resourceful British agent spins Fiona round at the precise moment the gun goes off and she receives the bullet intended for Bond.

ROSA KLEBB: Formerly a high ranking Soviet official, lesbian Rosa Klebb (Lotte Lenya) has joined SPECTRE by the time of the *From Russia With Love* operation. She uses her former position to fool unwitting Tatiana Romanova (Daniela Bianchi) by luring Bond into a devious SPECTRE plot. Klebb's shoes conceal poison-tipped spikes which she uses to good effect in the film.

Lenya is most impressive as the evil Klebb. This piece of casting, reputedly made by Harry Salzman, is one of the most successful of the series.

Miss Lenya died in 1981 aged 81. She was internationally revered as a legendary interpretor of the works of Bertolt Brecht and Kurt Weill. She was married to the latter.

KNOCKOUT: Bond is rendered unconscious at least once in every film. In two movies he suffers the ignominity of being knocked out more than once. This happens twice in *Diamonds Are Forever* and three times in *Goldfinger*. In all, 007 is rendered unconscious seventeen times in the series and on twelve of these occasions this is achieved by means of a blow to the back of the head by a villain's hand or the butt of his gun. A variation of this is the use of an ornamental trident wielded by Nick Nack (Herve Villechaize) in *The Man With The Golden Gun*.

Bond is also gassed twice – in *Diamonds Are Forever* while travelling in a lift and in *The Spy Who Loved Me* when Major Amasova (Barbara Bach) uses a cigarette, especially adapted for the purpose, during the boat trip down the River Nile.

007 is also shot by a tranquiliser gun in *Goldfinger*, beaten senseless in *Dr No* and passes out after crashing his Aston Martin DB5 in *Goldfinger*.

And the man still survives.

KRIEGLER: Ostensibly an East German defector, Kriegler (John Wyman) is in fact a KGB agent. In *For Your Eyes Only* he is the go-between in the recovery of the ATAC transmitter by Kristatos (Julian Glover) and its eventual delivery to General Gogol (Walter Gotell) of the KGB. In addition to his intelligence duties, Kriegler is a cross-country bi-athlon champion. He does not drink, smoke or talk to girls. He eats only health foods.

Kriegler is killed by Bond at the end of *For Your Eyes Only*. He is pushed backwards through a window in the mountaintop monastery of St Cyril's in Greece.

KRILENCU: A Bulgar used by Russians as a hit man in Istanbul is Krilencu (Fred Haggarty). Kerim Bey (Pedro Armendariz) warns 007 that he should remember Krilencu because the man 'kills for pleasure'. Krilencu masterminds the spectacular attack on the gipsy encampment in *From Russia With Love*. As retribution, 007 and Kerim tail him to his hideout. Kerim, despite a wounded arm, shoots Krilencu in the back as he attempts to escape from a window of a building. 'That settles many debts,' says Kerim.

KRISTATOS: Greek tycooon Kristatos (Julian Glover) is an anglophile considered to be a reliable secret service contact. But in *For Your Eyes Only* he turns out to be Bond's chief adversary. Kristatos is working on behalf of the Russians to retrieve the lost British transmitting device ATAC.

Kristatos has business interests which include shipping, insurance and oil exploration. His efforts for the Greek resistance during World War II earned him the King's Medal. He has a deceptively mild manner and seems to be genuine in his support for young ice skater and Olympic hopeful Bibi Dahl (Lynn-Holly Johnson). However, Kristatos is capable of great cruelty. Bond and Melina Havelock (Carole Bouquet) are keel-hauled on board Kristatos' yacht, the Santa Maura.

His great rival is Milos Columbo (Topol). Once they were like brothers, but this developed into only hate over the years. Although a KGB contact, Kristatos works only for money. With the ATAC in his hands, he intends to sell to the highest bidder. But Kristatos is killed by Columbo to prevent his great rival escaping with the vital device.

LADY-KILLER: Bond kills a woman intentionally only once in the series. This happens in *The Spy Who Loved Me*. 007, underwater in his aqua-Lotus Esprit, uses a missile to destroy the helicopter in which Stromberg's (Curt

Jurgens) assistant Naomi (Caroline Munro) has been chasing the British spy and his accomplice Major Anya Amasova (Barbara Bach).

PETER LAMONT: After beginning his long association with the Bond series as a draughtsman in the art department on *Goldfinger*, production designer Lamont has been employed on every Bond film since. He has progressed from chief draughtsman, through to assistant art director, set director and art director before becoming production designer from *For Your Eyes Only* onwards.

Lamont was nominated for an Oscar as art director on *The Spy Who Loved Me*.

EMILIO LARGO: Number two in the SPECTRE hierarchy, Emilio Largo (Adolfo Celi) is Blofeld's field commander when two atomic bombs are stolen from the NATO powers in *Thunderball*.

A large, gregarious character, Largo is piratical in his womanising and his wealth. He wears a black patch over his left eye. Largo is the owner of the Disco Volante, a yacht-cum-hydrofoil registered in Panama. Largo enjoys the underwater life. SPECTRE's number two is also guardian to Domino Derval (Claudine Auger). Largo is killed at the conclusion of *Thunderball* when 007 reaches the hydrofoil in time to prevent his adversary firing the atomic bombs.

LASER POWER: The first Bondian laser appears in *Goldfinger*. Lasers crop up in three Bond films and interestingly enough, the three films in which lasers appear correspond to the three films in which singer Shirley Bassey provides the theme song: *Goldfinger*, *Diamonds Are Forever* and *Moonraker*.

The laser which appears in *Goldfinger* was, at the time of the release of the film in 1964, an impossibility. Scientists had developed the theory but were not able to put this into practice and create a successful device. *Goldfinger* sees the laser used to threaten Bond, tied to the table in *Goldfinger's* (Gert Frobe) Swiss factory, Auric Enterprises. A laser is also used in the film's climax to burn the doors at Fort Knox.

Diamonds Are Forever features a laser built into an orbiting satellite. The aerofoils of the satellite are encrusted with diamonds which catch the sun to provide power. The satellite controlled by Blofeld (Charles Gray) is used to destroy major nuclear installations on earth. *Diamonds Are Forever* (1971) pre-dates Ronald Reagan's Star Wars programme by more than a decade.

Moonraker features hand-held lasers used at the film's climax during the assault on Hugo Drax's (Michael Lonsdale) space station. Drax's space shuttle – Moonraker 5 – is also equipped with a laser and is used by Bond to knock out the three nerve gas spheres launched by Drax before his demise.

LAZAR: Portuguese gun and bullet maker Lazar (Marne Maitland), is featured in *The Man With The Golden Gun*. Lazar is the supplier of Scaramanga's golden bullets which contain soft twenty-three-carat gold with traces of nickle, according to the evaluation of Q-branch.

When visited by Bond, Lazar shows a genuine pride in his work. He claims that he produces craftsmanship and quality. Lazar shows 007 the custom-built rifle he has just completed for a client, a man who has lost two fingers. To overcome this problem the trigger is housed in the butt. Bond says that the sights are not accurate but Lazar reminds Bond that he has five fingers and the rifle is balanced for the pressure of three.

Lazar sees himself performing his work with the skill and patience of a doctor or a priest with a penitent. But he tells 007 that bullets do not kill and adds that 'it is the finger that pulls the trigger'.

GEORGE LAZENBY: Following Sean Connery's refusal to continue with the Bond role after *You Only Live Twice*, Eon

Productions were forced to search for a new James Bond. Eventually, George Lazenby, an Australian male model who had arrived in England in 1964 and had appeared in Fry's Chocolate television commercials, was chosen by the producers who were impressed by his looks and his physique.

Lazenby's reign as 007 was brief. He made one film, *On Her Majesty's Secret Service*. Lazenby's problems seemed to stem from his inexperience and his age – it was his first screen role and he had little time to prepare. Lazenby was born in 1939. He was just twenty-nine when he made his first Bond film – making him rather young for Fleming's hero. Lazenby also had problems disguising his marked Australian accent which was not overcome by a crash course in elocution.

In spite of everything, *OHMSS* is regarded by many fans of the 007 series as the best in that it adheres most strongly to Fleming's book.

LE CERCLE: Bond is first introduced on screen at Le Cercle, Les Ambassadeurs Club, London. This casino sequence in *Dr No* sees Bond appear as a winner in a game of *chemin de fer* but before his face is seen. This is achieved by beating good-time girl Sylvia Trench (Eunice Gayson), the first woman 007 becomes romantically involved with on screen. The scene is rounded off nicely when Bond asks Sylvia, 'Do you play any other games?'

FELIX LEITER: *Dr No* sees the first appearance of American CIA agent Felix Leiter, played in the film by Jack Lord. The character takes a different actor with each new appearance in the series: *Goldfinger* (Cec Linder), *Thunderball* (Rik Van Nutter), *Diamonds Are Forever* (Norman Burton) and *Live And Let Die* (David Hedison). Hedison is a close friend of Roger Moore.

LEKTOR DECODER: The Russian decoding device, the Lektor decoder, with which SPECTRE intends to lure

James Bond to an ignominious death in *From Russia With Love* – is a lure that the British Secret Service cannot ignore, for both they and the CIA have been desperate to get their hands on the Lektor for years. The machine is about the size of a portable typewriter, is kept in a brown case and weighs ten kilos. During the course of the film, we learn that the Lektor possesses twenty-four single keys and sixteen coded keys. It is both self-calibrating and manual and has an inbuilt compensator. Tatiana Romanova (Daniela Bianchi) tells Bond that she once looked inside the Lektor when it was being repaired and saw many perforated disks inside, made, she thinks, of copper.

LENKIN: Kremlin Art Repository official Lenkin (Peter Porteous) is heavily involved in art treasure smuggling in *Octopussy*. Lenkin is answerable to General Orlov (Steven Berkoff), who, along with Prince Kamal Khan (Louis Jourdan) and Octopussy (Maud Adams), is stealing Soviet art treasures. Lenkin's participation in the caper is discovered when an unscheduled inventory of the repository reveals that the Romanoff Star, one of Russia's national treasures, is a fake.

LIPARUS: In *The Spy Who Loved Me*, Karl Stromberg (Curt Jurgens) uses the massive oil tanker Liparus to capture nuclear submarines. Naomi (Caroline Munro) tells Bond and Anya Amasova (Barbara Bach) about the Liparus, the latest addition to Stromberg's shipping fleet. She claims that the Liparus is the largest tanker in the world. But Anya disagrees and reminds Naomi that the Russian tanker, the Karl Marx, is larger.

Bond becomes suspicious of the Liparus and its movements. He discovers that in the nine months since the vessel was fitted out, there is no record of her having put into port.

To accommodate the interior of the Liparus – where three nuclear submarines are seen side by side –

production designer Ken Adam creates arguably his most impressive work of the series on the 007 stage at Pinewood Studios.

COUNT LIPPE: SPECTRE agent based at the Shrublands Health Clinic near a NATO airbase in Sussex is Count Lippe (Guy Doleman). Lippe, acting with Fiona (Luciana Paluzzi), oversees the substitution of the SPECTRE-manufactured double of Major Derval (Paul Stassino) for Angelo. Lippe is, or has been, a member of the Chinese Tong gang – a form of oriental Mafia – and Bond is alerted to this when he discovers the tell-tale mark of a Tong, a red square with a spike through it, on Count Lippe's wrist.

Lippe tries to kill Bond when he increases the speed of the traction device, The Rack, to which 007 is strapped to stretch the spine during his stay at the clinic.

Lippe is executed by his colleague because of his failure to kill 007. Fiona destroys Lippe's car by rockets fired from her motorcycle in an exciting car chase.

LISL: Mistress of Columbo (Topol) in *For Your Eyes Only*, Lisl, played by Australian actress Cassandra Harris, claims to be a countess. But a slip of the accent during a night-time rendezvous with 007 reveals that she hails from Liverpool.

Lisl invites 007 to her beach bungalow on Corfu for champagne and oysters. She is used by Columbo to investigate the activities of the agent. But after a night of passion, Lisl is killed when she and Bond are attacked by agents of Kristatos (Julian Glover). This beach scene has enemy agents (Michael Gothard and Charles Dance) driving dune buggies.

LITTLE NELLIE: Built in 1962, Little Nellie, the autogyro piloted by Bond in *You Only Live Twice* carried a dazzling array of weapons which all worked. The autogyro was equipped with flame and smoke generators, fourteen rockets in packs of seven, fifty parachute mines, two large guided weapons and two fixed machine guns which fired blanks.

Former RAF bomber Wing Commander Ken Wallis doubled for Connery in the aerial sequences. Wallis has to shave his moustache and wear an open-necked sleeveless shirt. His helmet was fitted with a dummy mine. Flights were made at an average of 6000 feet and his dress hardly suited the occasion. At times the cold was almost too much and the helmet made the autogyro unstable.

Little Nellie is fitted with a 1634cc much-modified target plane engine. The prototype was capable of a level speed of between 14 and 130 mph.

The name Little Nellie is a derivation of Wallis Autogyro – Nellie Wallace, hence, Little Nellie. Little Nellie still flies and is regularly seen at air displays up and down Britain.

Designed and built by the Wing Commander, who lives at Reymerston Hall, Norfolk, Little Nellie was first used in Army trials.

LIVE WIRES: Several characters suffer death or injury because of electrocution. Bond himself has received a shock on two occasions thanks to electricity. Once, nastily, when trying to break out of a cell in *Dr No* and again, rather less severely, in *OHMSS* when attempting to slip surreptitiously out of his room in Blofeld's (Telly Savalas) mountaintop fortress.

Two characters die as a result of electrocution in *Goldfinger*. The first is 007's attacker in the pre-credits sequence who perishes when Bond tosses an electric heater into the bath where he has just despatched his assailant after a fight. Oddjob (Harold Sakata), Goldfinger's henchman, dies in a vault at Fort Knox when 007 touches the exposed end of a severed cable to a metal grill. Oddjob's steel-rimmed hat is jammed in the grill. He dies as he attempts to retrieve it.

The unseen Blofeld of *Thunderball* eliminates a

treacherous member of SPECTRE at a Paris board meeting of the organisation. A massive current is passed through the man's chair. The equally anonymous Blofeld of the *For Your Eyes Only* pre-credits sequence murders the pilot of a helicopter ferrying Bond back to London headquarters by passing an electric current through the pilot's headphones.

Bond temporarily disables Jaws (Richard Kiel) during a fight on a train in *The Spy Who Loved Me*. 007 touches the massive killer's teeth with the shattered end of a broken table lamp. Jaws receives a considerable electric shock.

A minor character in the employ of Max Zorin (Christopher Walken) expires in a spectacular manner in *A View To A Kill*. He grabs hold of a fallen electric pylon during the destruction of the Main Strike Mine and is electrocuted.

EMILE LÉOPOLD LOCQUE: Enforcer in the Brussels underworld, Emile Léopold Locque (Michael Gothard) is the silent killer working for Kristatos (Julian Glover), Bond's chief adversary in *For Your Eyes Only*. Locque's file – displayed on the identigraph machine at Q-Branch, file number 5X10/459D7812F/DGB – shows that Locque has been convicted of several brutal murders.

He was imprisoned for life at Namur Prison in January 1975. But Locque escaped jail by strangling his psychiatrist. After that incident he was involved with drugs syndicates in Marseilles, Hong Kong and, latterly, Kristatos' operation in Greece.

Locque is killed in Albania when the car in which he has been chasing 007 crashes on to the edge of a precipice. The vehicle balances so precariously that it needs only a vicious kick from Bond to send it tumbling over the edge.

LONDON OPENING DATES: The opening dates for each film in James Bond's home town were:

Dr No   6th October 1962

From Russia With Love	10th October 1963
Goldfinger	17th September 1964
Thunderball	29th December 1965
You Only Live Twice	11th April 1967
On Her Majesty's Secret Service	18th December 1969
Diamonds Are Forever	30th December 1971
Live And Let Die	5th July 1973
The Man With The Golden Gun	19th December 1974
The Spy Who Loved Me	7th July 1977
Moonraker	26th June 1979
For Your Eyes Only	24th June 1981
Octopussy	6th June 1983
A View To A Kill	12th June 1985
The Living Daylights	29th June 1987

All but three of the Bond films have opened at The Odeon, Leicester Square in London. The three exceptions are *Dr No*, *From Russia With Love* and *Thunderball*, all of which opened at the London Pavilion.

The shortest gap between Bonds was that between *From Russia With Love* and *Goldfinger*, a period of eleven months. The longest was between *You Only Live Twice* and *OHMSS*, a gap of almost thirty-two months.

LOTUS CARS: Vehicles produced by the Norfolk-based sports car manufacturers Lotus Cars have appeared in two Bond films. *The Spy Who Loved Me* saw the introduction of a Lotus Esprit which, at a flick of a switch, transformed itself into a submarine. *For Your Eyes Only* featured two Lotus Esprit turbo sports cars.

During the filming of *The Spy Who Loved Me* Lotus provided seven body shells on set, one of which was converted by Perry Submarines into a submarine. This was piloted underwater by a stuntman in a wet suit.

The exploding Lotus in *For Your Eyes Only* featured a 'blow-up' car – a perfect replica of a Lotus Esprit minus an engine and much of the interior.

In addition to providing on-set technical back-up, Lotus Cars also helped supply extras on occasions. The firm's press officer, Don McLauchlan, stood in for Roger Moore during a brief sequence and Clive Chapman, son of Colin Chapman, the founder of Lotus Cars, featured as an extra in *For Your Eyes Only*.

'M': Admiral Sir Miles Messery KCMG, head of MI7 and known in the series as 'M', is almost as important a character as 007. For without 'M' to give the orders, there would be no missions for Bond to undertake.

Played with suitable crustiness by Bernard Lee for more than seventeen years, and played latterly by the slightly more paternal Robert Brown, 'M' is introduced to us at secret service headquarters in the initial sequences of *Dr No*.

The character of 'M' reflects perfectly the changing attitudes of British society, especially in the 1960s. 'M' represents the old order; Bond the new. There is a very definite barrier between the two men and 'M' frequently shows his detestation of Bond's casual attitude to service protocol.

'M' is the anchor man of the Bond series, rarely venturing out of his office until the fifth film, *You Only Live Twice*, when he and Miss Moneypenny (Lois Maxwell) appear in the Far East on board 'M''s personal submarine, M1. *For Your Eyes Only* is the only feature in which the character does not appear. Made just after the death of Bernard Lee, the film tells us that 'M' is 'on leave' and on this occasion the Chief Of Staff, Bill Tanner (James Villiers), deputises for him.

MI7: The department in which Bond works for British Intelligence is MI7. We learn at the beginning of *Dr No* that 'M' (Bernard Lee) is head of operations for MI7 and that since he took over the helm there has been a forty per cent drop in casualties.

McADAMS: Canadian chessmaster McAdams (Peter Maddern) is defeated by SPECTRE master planner Kronsteen (Vladek Sheybal) at a chess tournament in Venice early on in *From Russia With Love*.

MAC'S BACKTRACK: Patrick McGoohan, star of *Dangerman*, a popular television adventure series of the 1960s, was said to have turned down the opportunity to play Bond in *Dr No* because he objected to the role on moral grounds.

MAGDA: A charming lady in *Octopussy*, Magda (Kristina Wayborn) is heavily involved with the title character Octopussy (Maud Adams) and her partner-in-crime Prince Kamal Khan (Louis Jourdan). Miss Wayborn, a Swedish actress, won international acclaim in the role of Greta Garbo in the Moviola mini-series on television.

MAGNETIC PULSE: The magnetic pulse of a nuclear explosion is enough to disable all microchips in the Bondian world prior to *A View To A Kill*. As Bond explains to the Minister of Defence, following a burst of a nuclear explosion in space over the United Kingdom, everything with a microchip in it, from the modern toaster to Britain's defence systems, would be rendered absolutely useless. That is the reason why a private defence contractor is asked to come up with a chip which is totally impervious to magnetic pulse damage – a company which is acquired by Zorin Industries, thus enabling the KGB to get a pipeline into the firm and acquire the new microchip technology. It is this fact that leads Bond on to the trail of Max Zorin (Christopher Walken) and begins the perilous mission that is *A View To A Kill*.

MAGNIFICENT 007: Scenes in *Moonraker* showing Bond disguised as a gaucho – in the Clint Eastwood 'man with no name' mould – are accompanied on the soundtrack by an arrangement of Elmer Bernstein's theme from *The Magnificent Seven*.

RICHARD MAIBAUM: Veteran American screenwriter Maibaum was born in 1909. He has been the most prolific writer on the series over the past twenty-five years. He has written or co-written *Dr No, From Russia With Love, Goldfinger, Thunderball, OHMSS, Diamonds Are Forever, The Man With The Golden Gun, The Spy Who Loved Me, For Your Eyes Only, Octopussy, A View To A Kill* and *The Living Daylights*.

Maibaum began writing scrips for Hollywood films in the mid-1930s, by which time he was already an established stage actor, producer and playwright. He first became associated with Cubby Broccoli in the mid-1950s during the making of *The Red Beret*.

MAINSTRIKE MINE: The Mainstrike Mine is the focal point of Max Zorin's (Christopher Walken) evil designs in *A View To A Kill*. The abandoned silver mine lies near the San Andreas Fault in California. Zorin hopes to create a double earthquake by blasting away the geological lock which prevents the San Andreas Fault and the Haywards Fault moving at once. In this way he hopes to manipulate the earth's crusts to flood Silicon Valley in the 'greatest cataclysm in history'.

MAKING TRACKS: Bond films have used the confined space provided on trains as the backdrop for some of the most spectacular action scenes. *From Russia With Love* features one of the best remembered, when Bond tackles SPECTRE's Donald Grant (Robert Shaw) on board the Orient Express.

The closing action in *Live And Let Die* sees 007 and Solitaire (Jane Seymour) intercepted by a revenge-seeking Tee Hee (Julius W. Harris), a henchman of the late Mr Big (Yaphet Kotto). This gives Bond a few anxious moments but Tee Hee is flipped out of the window of a moving train by the British Agent.

Jaws (Richard Kiel) attacks Anya Amasova (Barbara Bach) in *The Spy Who Loved Me* aboard a train, and this alerts Bond to his presence. During the course of the ensuing fight, 007 is thrown around the carriage by his adversary. But Bond manages to electrocute Jaws when he touches the villain's steel teeth with a broken lamp, stunning the giant long enough to push him through a window.

Octopussy has Bond, in disguise, discovering the true nature of General Orlov's (Steven Berkoff) plot. The subsequent battles above, and below, a speeding train make for exciting viewing.

Bond takes the underground in *You Only Live Twice*. Tiger Tanaka (Tetsuro Tamba), head of the Japanese Secret Service, travels through Tokyo on his own private underground train. He tells 007 that it is too dangerous for him to travel the streets.

MAKING WAVES: *Dr No* ends with Bond and Honey Rider (Ursula Andress) aboard a boat after Dr No's complex at Crab Key had been destroyed. A precedent is set here. Most Bond films end in this fashion with the hero and leading lady entwined in each other's arms on a boat. This happens again in *From Russia With Love, Thunderball, You Only Live Twice, Diamonds Are Forever, The Man With The Golden Gun, The Spy Who Loved Me, For Your Eyes Only* and *Octopussy*.

TOM MANKIEWICZ: American screenwriter Tom Mankiewicz was credited as a screenwriter on three Bonds: *Diamonds Are Forever; The Man With The Golden Gun*, which he wrote with Richard Maibaum, and *Live And Let Die*.

MARRIAGE: Bond marries only once in the series, but the various writers engaged in creating 007's screen adventures have been unable to resist the idea of a Mrs Bond on several occasions.

Bond marries Tracy Vincenzo (Diana Rigg) in *OHMSS* only to lose his wife less than an hour after the ceremony, during the reception, to a hail of bullets fired by Blofeld's

(Telly Savalas) evil helper Irma Bunt (Ilse Steppat). Bond and Tatiana Romanova (Daniela Bianchi) pose as a married couple in *From Russia With Love*. They call themselves David and Caroline Somerset, of Derbyshire, to cover their escape on the Orient Express.

Bond takes part in a mock wedding ceremony with Kissy Suzuki (Mie Hama) in *You Only Live Twice*, as part of his cover to seek out Blofeld's (Donald Pleasence) activities.

The Spy Who Loved Me has Bond and Major Anya Amasova (Barbara Bach) posing as husband and wife marine biologists, Mr and Mrs Robert Stirling, to gain entrance to Karl Stromberg's (Curt Jurgens) Atlantis stronghold.

In *Live And Let Die*, Bond arrives at his hotel on the Caribbean island of San Monique and is informed that 'Mrs Bond' has already checked in. Mrs Bond turns out to be Rosie Carver (Gloria Hendry), ostensibly a CIA agent assigned to Bond but later 007 finds out that she is working for Mr Big (Yaphet Kotto).

MARVELLOUS MARVIN: The soundtrack of *The Spy Who Loved Me*, the tenth Eon Bond film, was written by Marvin Hamlisch, the Oscar-winning composer.

Hamlisch, who also wrote music for *The Sting* and *The Way We Were*, wrote a score that superbly underlined the action and spectacle of *The Spy Who Loved Me*. He also wrote the theme song 'Nobody Does It Better', sung by American songstress, Carly Simon. The lyrics were by Carole Bayer Sager. The theme song was a huge hit worldwide and Hamlisch's score was nominated for an Oscar.

THE MASTERSONS: Jill and Tilly Masterson (Shirley Eaton and Tania Mallett) are sisters who meet death because of their involvement with master villain, Goldfinger (Gert Frobe). Jill is a companion for Goldfinger. She is paid to be seen in public with him. She helps Goldfinger in his cheating at cards against Simmons (Austin Willis) in an early scene in the holiday setting of Miami Beach.

But Jill pays for her alliance with Bond. He puts a stop to her fun by having her covered from head to toe in gold paint. Jill dies of skin suffocation

Her sister vows to avenge Jill's death. Tilly tails Goldfinger to Switzerland where she aims to kill him. Here she runs into Bond. But she meets her end at the hands of Oddjob (Harold Sakata) and his hat with the razor-sharp band.

MATT FINISH: Matt Monro's vocal version of the theme to *From Russia With Love*, of the same name, is unusually held back from the film's titles. Instead of the song, the film's credits are accompanied by an instrumental. We are introduced to the theme song when it is briefly heard coming from a radio. Bond and Sylvia Trench (Eunice Gayson) – Bond's first dalliance with Sylvia was in *Dr No* – are relaxing in a punt by the river. The theme is heard in full over the film's final credits.

MAX: A colourful parrot, Max is the constant companion of marine archaeologist and British agent Sir Timothy Havelock (Jack Hedley) for more than thirty years. The voice of the parrot is provided by animal mimic Percy Edwards. Max, who appears in *For Your Eyes Only*, unwittingly leads Bond to the ATAC transmitter. Max also gets to chat to Prime Minister Margaret Thatcher (Janet Brown) over a radio telephone link in the film's irreverent but funny tag scene.

MAY DAY: Whether dressed from head to toe in black leather, or else wearing naught but a tight leotard, the striking black fantasy figure of May Day is the undisputed symbol of *A View To A Kill*.

As both bodyguard and lover to villain Max Zorin (Christopher Walken), May Day is without doubt the most extraordinary physical creation ever seen in any Bond film.

Played by model and rock star Grace Jones, the character of May Day clearly demonstrates that she is no ordinary woman. She teaches Max Zorin how to kick-box and can effortlessly lift KGB agent Klotkoff (Bogdan Kominowski) above her head. As Grace Jones was quoted as saying at the release of the film, May Day was to be the definitive Bond villainess – killing in a very stylish, sexy, feminine, but nasty manner. The look for the character – based on the idea of a silhouette – was a direct collaboration between Jones, her personal costume designer, Azzedine Alaia, and *A View To A Kill*'s costume designer, Emma Porteous.

MERIT HONOUR: For his efforts in frustrating Max Zorin's (Christopher Walken) evil plans in *A View To A Kill*, Bond – in his absence – is awarded the order of Lenin by the Kremlin. This is the Soviet Union's highest honour and we are told that 007 is the first non-Soviet citizen to receive the award.

METZ: Leading world expert in light refraction and committed idealist, Dr Metz (Joseph Furst) is duped into building the diamond-encrusted super laser in *Diamonds Are Forever*. Dr Metz believes that the device will be used only to destroy nuclear installations and weapons.

Blofeld tells the good doctor that they have a common goal – disarmament and world peace – but Blofeld's real aim is an international auction with nuclear supremacy going to the highest bidder. Dr Metz is presumed killed in the helicopter attack on Blofeld's oil rig headquarters at the conclusion of *Diamonds Are Forever*.

MOJAVE CLUB: Bond meets Russian agent Anya Amasova (Barbara Bach) in the Mojave Club, Cairo. The nightclub is owned by Max Kalba (Vernon Dobcheff). 007 and Amasova attempt to outbid each other for the microfilm copy of a submarine tracking system, in this scene from *The Spy Who Loved Me*. The original soundtrack album of the film features a track written by Marvin Hamlisch, titled the Mojave Club. This music accompanies the scenes at the club.

MISS MONEYPENNY: Private secretary and personal assistant to the head of the British Secret Service, 'M', Miss Moneypenny (Lois Maxwell) was a permanent fixture in the first fourteen films. Since *Dr No* she has lavished much love and attention on the amorous secret agent, but her advances were all to no avail. Always the bridesmaid and never the bride, the scenes between Bond and Moneypenny were always a memorable feature of the series.

For twenty-three years the Canadian actress played the part and is the only person to appear in the first fourteen films.

Miss Maxwell made her Hollywood debut in 1947, co-starring with Shirley Temple in *That Hagen Girl*. The film also featured US president Ronald Reagan. Miss Maxwell is a keen writer and has contributed a daily newspaper column, entitled 'Moneypenny', in her home town of Toronto.

The key relationship between 007 and Moneypenny was established by Sean Connery and Miss Maxwell early on during the filming of *Dr No*. They decided that they would play their roles as if Bond and Moneypenny had once enjoyed a brief fling many years earlier, thus creating the characters' mutual affection.

Lois Maxwell made her last appearance as Moneypenny in Roger Moore's final Bond, *A View To A Kill*, in 1985. The role is taken by Caroline Bliss in *The Living Daylights*.

MONOGRAM FEATURES: Only once has James Bond been seen to wear an item of clothing bearing a monogram. The initials JB are seen on the dressing gown he wears in *Live And Let Die*. This is the first and the last time that the dressing gown is featured.

An item of equipment issued to Bond bearing his

unique stamp is the miniature camera in *Moonraker* used to photograph the contents of Hugo Drax's (Michael Lonsdale) safe. The camera bears the inscription '007'. The camera lens is housed behind the second 0 of the agent's number.

ROGER MOORE: Following George Lazenby's ineffectual performance in *OHMSS* and Sean Connery's one-off return in *Diamonds Are Forever*, it was announced on August 1st 1972 at the Dorchester Hotel, London, that Roger Moore was to be the next James Bond.

Moore, the son of a Stockwell police sergeant, was born on October 14th 1927. His first screen work was as an extra in *Caesar and Cleopatra* in 1945. The co-director of the film, Brian Desmond Hurst, saw potential in young Moore. Hurst paid Moore's fees at the Royal Academy of Dramatic Art. Moore's first film was MGM's *The Last Time I Saw Paris* which starred Elizabeth Taylor. He stayed in the States for television series which included *The Alaskans*, *Ivanhoe* and *Maverick*.

Then came *The Saint* in 1962. Lew Grade had bought the rights to the adventure serial from Leslie Charteris and thought Moore was perfect for the role of the Saint – a part which he stayed with for seven years.

After *The Saint*, Moore vowed that he would never make another television series. He moved back into feature films which included *Crossplot* and *The Man Who Haunted Himself*. But Grade persuaded Moore to co-star opposite Tony Curtis in *The Persuaders*.

Roger Moore became James Bond in his 46th year, the oldest actor to play the part. He made seven 007 films, the same number as Sean Connery. They were: *Live And Let Die*, *The Man With The Golden Gun*, *The Spy Who Loved Me*, *Moonraker*, *For Your Eyes Only*, *Octopussy* and *A View To A Kill*. Moore's twelve-year reign as Bond is the longest.

TED MOORE: South African born cinematographer Ted Moore added his expertise to good effect in *Dr No*, *From*

Russia With Love, Goldfinger, Thunderball, Diamonds Are Forever and *The Man With The Golden Gun.*

CARL MORTNER: Ostensibly Max Zorin's (Christopher Walken) horse breeding consultant, Dr Carl Mortner (Willoughby Gray) is close to Zorin in his activities. Mortner's real name is Hans Glaub. During World War II he was a German pioneer in the development of steroids. We are told he experimented with pregnant women in concentration camps in an attempt to stimulate intelligence in unborn children.

Most women miscarried and those children that survived were blessed with a phenomenal IQ, but there were psychotic side effects. Zorin was one of the youngsters to survive.

At the end of the war the Soviets captured Mortner. He was set up in a laboratory to produce steroids for athletes. But Mortner disappeared in the late 1960s – about the same time Zorin defected to the West from East Germany.

Mortner dies at the conclusion of *A View To A Kill* when Zorin's airship explodes high above San Francisco's Golden Gate Bridge.

MOUNT TOFANA: A mountain near Cortina, northern Italy, 3242 metres above sea level, is Mount Tofana. The mountain is used as a rendezvous for Bond and Ferrara (John Moreno), a British secret service agent, in *For Your Eyes Only.*

SIR DONALD MUNGER: First to alert the British Government to diamond smuggling activities in *Diamonds Are Forever* is Sir Donald Munger (Laurence Naismith), head of the London-based diamond syndicate. This leads Bond and the secret service to Blofeld's (Charles Gray) trail.

NAME GAME: Bond uses several aliases. He travels to

Jamaica in *Dr No* under the cover of a representative of Universal Exports. *From Russia With Love* sees 007 and Tatiana (Daniela Bianchi) travelling under the cover of David and Caroline Somerset, returning home to Derbyshire. 007 poses as Mr Fisher – managing director of Empire Chemicals – in *You Only Live Twice*. *OHMSS* sees Bond assume not only the name but the identity of Sir Hilary Bray.

In *Diamonds Are Forever*, 007 uses the identity of diamond smuggler Peter Franks (Joe Robinson) to penetrate the diamond smuggling pipeline between Amsterdam and Los Angeles. 007 poses as marine biologist Robert Stirling in *The Spy Who Loved Me* in order to gain entrance to Karl Stromberg's (Curt Jurgens) marine fortress.

Bond enters East Germany as Charles Morton, a manufacturer's representative from Leeds, visiting a furniture warehouse in the Eastern Block, in *Octopussy*. In *A View To A Kill*, 007 assumes two false identities – wealthy horse breeder James St John Smythe and *Financial Times* reporter James Stock.

NAOMI: A female receptionist employed by Stromberg (Curt Jurgens) in *The Spy Who Loved Me*, Naomi is played by Caroline Munro. Naomi is based at Atlantis, Stromberg's underwater stronghold off the coast of Sardinia. Bond and Anya Amasova (Barbara Bach) are shown around Atlantis by Naomi. The couple are posing as marine biologists Robert Stirling and his wife.

Naomi is a qualified helicopter pilot and it is she who takes control of the machine-gun-firing helicopter that pursues Bond and Anya in the Lotus Esprit, along the isolated roads of Sardinia. Naomi is killed by Bond when he brings down her helicopter by means of a missile fired from the Lotus.

NEVER SAY NEVER AGAIN: The second non-Eon produced Bond film, *Never Say Never Again*, was released in 1983. This picture marked the return of Sean Connery to the role of 007 – twelve years after his final Eon appearance in *Diamonds Are Forever*.

Never Say Never Again was produced by Jack Schwartman and Kevin McClory. The latter owns rights to the story of *Thunderball* of which this new film is a remake. *Never Say Never Again* is a better film than *Casino Royale* but is nevertheless disappointing.

Directed by Irvin Kershner of *The Empire Strikes Back* fame, the film suffers from a confused and lack-lustre script, a dreary score and flat production values.

NICK NACK: Diminutive French actor Hervé Villechaize contributes the character of Nick Nack in *The Man With The Golden Gun*. Nick Nack is assistant to Scaramanga (Christopher Lee). A cordon bleu chef who also enjoys peanuts, Nick Nack is a grotesque figure – never more so than in the scenes when he is serving wine or champagne. He becomes the nightmarish parody of the perfect waiter and, despite being a little less than four feet high, Villechaize almost steals the picture from the principals in the cast.

NING-PO: Registered in Shanghai, the vessel Ning-po belongs to Osato Chemicals and Engineering and is the means of transporting fuel for Blofeld's (Donald Pleasence) rocket interceptor in *You Only Live Twice*. The Ning-po is taking on supplies of liquid oxygen at Kobe Docks, Japan, when it is investigated by Bond and Aki (Akiko Wakabayashi). This leads to an attack by Mr Osato's (Teru Shimada) men and Bond's brief capture by SPECTRE number eleven, Helga (Karin Dor).

NINJAS: *You Only Live Twice* features Tiger Tanaka's (Tetsuro Tamba) top secret force of Ninja warriors. The Ninjas are a force trained in the art of concealment and surprise. Tanaka runs a Ninja training school in the shadow of an impressive Japanese castle. The Ninjas are skilled in the art of hand-to-hand combat but are not averse to using modern weapons technology.

The Ninjas help Bond at the conclusion of the film when 007 enters Blofeld's (Donald Pleasence) volcano base to foil a possible World War III.

NO YOLK: A gloriously decorated, jewelled Fabergé egg leads Bond to the trail of Prince Kamal Khan (Louis Jourdan) in *Octopussy*. Fabergé eggs were created for the Russian Czars and given as Easter gifts. The sale of a Fabergé egg at Sotheby's auction rooms coincides with the discovery of a deceased 009 (Andy Bradford) clutching a near-perfect forgery. The sale of the egg, entitled the 'Property of a Lady', is a nice touch. This was the title of a short story published by Fleming under the umbrella heading of *Octopussy*.

NUCLEAR POWER: Nuclear power is mentioned in *Dr No* and reappears, whether as a good or bad force, in *Goldfinger*, *Thunderball*, *OHMSS*, *Dimaonds Are Forever*, *The Spy Who Loved Me*, *For Your Eyes Only* and *Octopussy*.

NUCLEAR WEAPONS: Nuclear weapons feature in five films: *Goldfinger*, *Thunderball*, *Diamonds Are Forever*, *The Spy Who Loved Me* and *Octopussy*. Sixteen Polaris missiles are captured from a British submarine by Karl Stromberg (Curt Jurgens) in *The Spy Who Loved Me*. An American missile silo and a number of Chinese nuclear missiles are destroyed by Blofeld's (Charles Gray) laser satellite in *Diamonds Are Forever*.

Auric Goldfinger (Gert Frobe) chains Bond to a nuclear bomb in the vaults of Fort Knox. This is a huge affair which resembles a metal crate and inside is a mass of complicated electronics. But the nuclear bomb primed for detonation at a USAF base in *Octopussy* is much smaller. This bomb is Soviet made and resembles an American medium yield bomb. The plot in *Octopussy* revolves around the need to convince the world that an American bomb has been triggered accidently.

The *Thunderball* plot concentrates on SPECTRE's theft from a Vulcan bomber of two nuclear warheads. The bombs – MOS type, numbers 456 and 457 – are put up to ransom for a hundred million pounds. The weapons are black with rounded noses. 'Handle like eggs' is written on the side.

OCE: Osato Chemicals and Engineering, based in Tokyo and owned by Mr Osato (Teru Shimada), is the cover for SPECTRE's space capsule stealing conspiracy in *You Only Live Twice*. OCE, we are told, is one of the largest industrial concerns in Japan. The business provides Blofeld (Donald Pleasence) with men and equipment to operate the rocket base hidden in the crater of an extinct volcano.

OCTOPUS TATTOO: A tattoo of an octopus is a trait of the female employees of Octopussy (Maud Adams). A blue-ringed octopus is the sign of an ancient secret order of female bandits and smugglers. The cult is revived by Octopussy for her own band of female smugglers.

OCTOPUSSY: Maud Adams' Octopussy is the only female character to take the title role in the series. Octopussy is a wealthy woman living on an island off the coast of India populated exclusively by women. No one knows Octopussy's real name, but it transpires that Bond has had connections with her family in the past. Octopussy's father, Major Dexter-Smythe, was seconded to the British Secret Service after a brilliant military career. He was detailed to recover a cache of Chinese gold in North Korea. Instead of delivering the gold, Dexter-Smythe killed his guide and disappeared with his bounty. Twenty years later, Bond was sent out to find the missing major after the guide's body was discovered. A bullet in the guide's skull was identified as coming from Dexter-Smythe's revolver. Bond tracked down the Major in Sri Lanka and faced him with the facts. Dexter-Smythe was given twenty-four hours to clear up his affairs before 007 took him back to Britain. But rather than face the ignominy of a court martial, the Major shot himself.

During the enforced exile in Sri Lanka, Dexter-Smythe became a leading authority on octopi. Hence, his pet name for his daughter was Octopussy.

When her father's gold ran out, Octopussy was offered a commission to smuggle diamonds for the people who disposed of Dexter-Smythe's gold on the open market. She informs Bond that she discovered she had a talent for smuggling. Octopussy went into business by herself, reviving an old Octopus cult and recruiting young women from all over South East Asia to join in her bandit operations.

Octopussy also diversified into shipping, hotels, the circus and carnival entertainment but retained her links with smuggling. When Bond encounters her, she is involved in a scheme to steal art treasures from the vaults of the Kremlin with Prince Kamal Khan (Louis Jourdan) and General Orlov (Steven Berkoff).

Maud Adams is the only actress to make a return in a starring role in the series. She had previously played Andrea Anders in *The Man With The Golden Gun*.

ODDJOB: Played by Harold Sakata, Oddjob in *Goldfinger* is the blueprint for the Bondian bodyguard and thug – a tough, seemingly indestructable barrier between 007 and his chief adversary. Oddjob is a formal servant employed by Goldfinger (Gert Frobe). A mute, he goes about his work with deadly efficiency. Though his appearance is made to look fairly ridiculous with the addition of a bowler hat which conceals a metal rim. Oddjob is adept at breaking an opponent's neck with this nasty device. This fate befalls Tilly Masterson (Tania Mallet).

Sakata, a professional wrestler, died in 1982 aged sixty-two.

The character inspired the likes of Tee-Hee (Julius W. Harris), Nick Nack (Hervé Villechaize), Jaws (Richard Kiel), Gobinda (Kabir Bedi) and May Day (Grace Jones).

OILS WELL?: Bob Conley, (Manning Redwood) Max Zorin's (Christopher Walken) geologist who runs the Zorin Oil Reclamation project in *A View To A Kill*, is a man with a shady past. Conley was forced to leave his previous job under a cloud. Chief engineer at a South American gold mine, Conley departed from his work in a hurry when a cave-in killed twenty miners.

Conley's contribution to Project Mainstrike is to oversee the pumping of sea water into the geological faults around the Mainstrike mine in California. But on the completion of his work he is callously murdered by Zorin and head of security Scarpine (Patrick Bauchau) along with the rest of the workforce. Zorin intends that few people should have knowledge of his activities in Silicon Valley.

OOPS: *Thunderball* is the Bond film to suffer most from continuity errors. The most notorious is Domino's (Claudine Auger) shoulder strap which somehow appears intact just a moment after having been torn open by Largo (Adolfo Celi).

OPERATION BEDLAM: The code word for the intense search for Blofeld (Donald Pleasence) which began at the end of *You Only Live Twice* and continued at the outset of *OHMSS* is Operation Bedlam. This operation leads to a great degree of friction between 007, who is adamant that the search should continue, and 'M' (Bernard Lee) who is equally adamant that the operation be called off.

OPERATION KID BROTHER: A curious Italian attempt to jump on the Bond bandwagon in 1967 was a film entitled Operation Kid Brother. According to the plot, 007's younger brother defeats a criminal mastermind with the help of an archery team from Scotland. Sean Connery's brother Neil stars in the picture. Bondian stalwarts Bernard Lee and Lois Maxwell were somehow persuaded to appear along with Adolfo Celi and Daniela Bianchi, familiar faces to 007 fans. Alberto de Martinio directed the adventure which was described by the *Monthly Film Bulletin* as 'bad enough to be hysterically funny.'

OPERATION ORCHID: Hugo Drax's (Michael Lonsdale) bid to destroy humanity by launching globes of highly toxic nerve gas, derived from the rare orchid Orchidaceae Negra, from his orbiting space station is code-named Operation Orchid. This attack is set to take place from the Moonraker space station.

OPERATION PASSOVER: The CIA-run operation in *Diamonds Are Forever* to transfer 50,000 carats of diamonds to Tiffany Case (Jill St John) in New York is code-named Operation Passover.

OPERATION ROCKABYE BABY: Aimed at disabling 41,000 troops stationed at Fort Knox, Operation Rockabye Baby is a prelude to Operation Fort Knox, the assault on Fort Knox featured in *Goldfinger*. Rockabye Baby is the code-name used by Goldfinger (Gert Frobe) for the spraying of Delta 9 nerve gas in the vicinity of the complex. This work is carried out by Pussy Galore's (Honor Blackman) Flying Circus in the Piper Cherokee aircraft.

OPERATION TROVE: The mission to investigate the mysterious death of 009 (Andy Bradford) in *Octopussy* is given the code-name Operation Trove. 009 is found dead clutching a fake Fabergé egg.

OPERATION UNDERTOW: The code-name for the British Secret Service mission to locate and retrieve the automatic Targetting Attack Communicator device in *For Your Eyes Only* is Operation Undertow.

ORCHIDACEAE NEGRA: An essential element in the nerve gas manufactured by Hugo Drax (Michael Lonsdale) in *Moonraker* is Orchidaceae Negra. This very rare orchid, once thought to be extinct, was found by a missionary in an area of the River Topirapi in the upper reaches of the Amazoco in South America. We are told that in the past, tribes in South America have been wiped out by their reverence for the orchid because long-term exposure to its pollen causes sterility. As Bond discovers, Drax has improved upon sterility. Instead, a highly toxic nerve gas is produced which kills humans but has little effect on other animal life or plants.

GENERAL ORLOV: A renegade Russian General and one of the chief protagonists in *Octopussy*, General Orlov is played by actor, writer and director Steven Berkoff. General Orlov is a member of the supreme policy making council of the Soviet Union. He is regarded as one of the 'hawks' in the Soviet Union. But his patriotism does not extend to her art treasures. He is deeply involved with Octopussy (Maud Adams) and Prince Kamal Khan (Louis Jourdan) in a devious plot to substitute Kremlin art treasure for forgeries and sell the genuine article in the West.

Under his command in East Germany, Orlov has thirty-one divisions. This includes eleven tank divisions. There are also five more divisions under his control in Czechoslovakia and in support on the Russian border are another sixty divisions including a further twenty-two tank divisions. In all, Orlov has a ten to one advantage over NATO forces in Europe.

Orlov's death is ironic. He is killed on the East-West border by East German guards who think he is trying to defect. But his real intention is to thwart Bond who has discovered Orlov's plot.

Steven Berkoff is the founder of the London Theatre Group.

PLENTY O'TOOLE: Good-time girl Plenty O'Toole (Lana Wood – sister of Natalie) meets Bond in a Las Vegas gambling joint while 007 is posing as diamond smuggler

Peter Franks in this scene from *Diamonds Are Forever*. Plenty O'Toole – 'named after your father,' comments Bond – is murdered by gangsters loyal to Blofeld (Charles Gray) who mistake her for Tiffany Case (Jill St John).

OUR MAN IN…: During the scene in *Goldfinger* when Bond survives his encounter with the laser, Bond reveals that if he fails to report to headquarters, 008 will be sent out to replace him. This is the first mention of other 00 agents and it is not to be the last.

During the Thunderball affair, every 00 agent in Europe is called to headquarters in London and we see them together during a briefing session. In *The Man With The Golden Gun* we are told that Scaramanga (Christopher Lee) killed Bill Fairbanks, 002, in Beirut in 1969. The murder of 009 at the beginning of *Octopussy* launches 007 on a perilous mission. In *A View To A Kill* we see 003's frozen body. 004 is killed in Gibraltar in *The Living Daylights*.

OUT ON A LIMB: A crocodile named Albert is one of hundreds guarding Mr Big's (Yaphet Kotto) farm in *Live And Let Die* where heroin-refining labs are hidden. Tee-Hee (Julius W. Harris) tells Bond that he got careless some time ago with Albert and the crocodile took his right arm off. Tee-Hee is forced to rely upon a metallic arm and claw.

PARACHUTES: In keeping with the Bond producers' liking for aerial sequences to provide excitement, parachutes have appeared in many of the Bond films.

Goldfinger ends with Bond and Pussy Galore (Honor Blackman), entwined in the folds of a parachute, having narrowly missed being killed when Goldfinger's private Lockheed Jet Star plane crashes into the sea. In *Thunderball*, the US Marines parachute into the water to intercept the team of SPECTRE frogmen who are transporting one of the stolen atomic bombs to Miami which is to be the first target.

To confront Ernst Stavro Blofeld (Charles Gray), in *Diamonds Are Forever*, Bond flies out to Blofeld's oil-rig and parachutes into the sea protected in a silver balloon which is captured by Blofeld's men.

The pre-credits sequences of *The Spy Who Loved Me* and *Moonraker* feature parachutes. In *The Spy Who Loved Me*, Bond escapes his KGB attackers in Austria by ski-ing over a cliff and uses a Union Jack parachute to float to safety. *Moonraker* opens with Bond attacked aboard a plane by the crew, one of whom is pushed out wearing a parachute. Bond is then pushed out by Jaws (Richard Kiel) without a parachute. Bond escapes by manoeuvring himself in the air so that he intercepts the other man and steals the parachute from him.

In *A View To A Kill*, Bond pursues May Day (Grace Jones) to the top of the Eiffel Tower, only to see her jump and float away beneath a parachute. 007 also uses a parachute in *The Living Daylights*.

PARIS: The capital city of France has been used twice as a location for the Bond films and once as a studio base.

In *Thunderball*, SPECTRE has its secret headquarters in a fashionable street not far from the Eiffel Tower. It operates under a charitable front, the International Brotherhood for Stateless Persons. SPECTRE Number Two, Emilio Largo (Adolfo Celi), is well known by the city's police force. When he parks his car on the street outside the Brotherhood's offices, a traffic policeman ticks him off ... until he sees that it is Largo and then he salutes and says: 'Oh, pardon Monsieur Largo.'

A View To A Kill has more extensive scenes set in Paris. Following a lead, Bond meets with a private investigator, Aubergene (Jean Rougerie), and dines with him in a fashionable restaurant atop the Eiffel Tower. It is here that Aubergene is murdered by May Day (Grace Jones) and, in the ensuing chase, May Day parachutes out of reach of a pursuing Bond. The parachute jump was made by B. J. Worth, an American parachute specialist and a man who had performed aerial stunts on *Moonraker* and *Octopussy*.

When *Moonraker* was filmed in 1979, a combination of costs and taxation in Britain at that time necessitated Eon Productions to move away from their traditional base at Pinewood Studios – although some special effects were completed there – to three studios near Paris, where the extensive, futuristic sets depicting the world of Hugo Drax were constructed.

PASS-WORDS: The Secret Service uses a variety of recognition codes between agents throughout the Bond series. In *From Russia With Love* there appears the most complicated code:

Agent 1: 'Excuse me, do you have a match?'

Agent 2: 'I use a lighter.'

Agent 1: 'Better still.'

Agent 2: 'Until they go wrong.'

The pass-word in *You Only Live Twice* is much simpler – 'I love you'. In *The Spy Who Loved Me*, Bond cannot even trust his old school friend, Sheik Hossein (Edward de Souza), without an exchange of codes. When Bond, himself disguised as a sheik, arrives at Hossein's sumptuous tent, the conversation goes as follows: Bond – 'May the peace of Allah descend upon the magnificent abode and allow a poor traveller to enter.' Hossein – 'And may the hospitality of these miserable quarters be sufficient to your honoured needs.'

For Your Eyes Only has yet another recognition exchange:

Agent 1: 'The snow this year is better at Innsbruck.'

Agent 2: 'But not at St Moritz.'

Octopussy features a humorous code. When Bond first arrives in India, an agent of Station 1, Vijay (Vijay Armstrong), is disguised as a snake charmer. Spying Bond, Vijay's flute emits a couple of bars of the James Bond Theme and, as Bond stops and approaches, 007 says: 'That's a charming tune. You do take English money?'

In *A View To A Kill*, Bond identifies himself to Chuck Lee (David Yip), a CIA agent in San Francisco's Chinatown. Lee, under-cover, disguised as a helper on a shell-fish stall, is asked for soft-shell crabs.

PAULA: Bond's helper in Nassau during the *Thunderball* affair is Paula, played by Martine Beswick, an actress making her return to the series following her appearance as one of the fighting gypsy girls in *From Russia With Love*.

In *Thunderball*, her role is a greater one than in her previous Bond film. She appears in several scenes with Sean Connery, most notably during the sequence when Bond first makes contact with Domino Derval (Claudine Auger).

Paula's fate in *Thunderball* is to be captured by SPECTRE's killer, Fiona (Luciana Paluzzi) and SPECTRE agents. Ensconced in an escape-proof cellar at Palmyra, Emilio Largo's luxurious residence in the Bahamas, Paula takes poison rather than submit to questioning.

PAWS FOR THOUGHT: The white cat owned by Ernst Stavro Blofeld has appeared in virtually every scene in which the character of Blofeld appears. The cat plays an important part in character identification in that it becomes a characteristic of Blofeld.

Thus, in *From Russia With Love* and *Thunderball*, when Blofeld's face is not seen and he is referred to as Number

One, the camera concentrates upon the face of the cat to generate a sinister image. Similarly, in *You Only Live Twice*, when Blofeld is seen for the first time – played by Donald Pleasence – the film-makers are able to use the cat to build audience expectation until the final revelation of Blofeld.

Such is the part that Blofeld's cat plays in the early films – five appearances in the first seven epics – that title designer Maurice Binder includes shots of the cat, with a diamond-encrusted collar, in the credits of *Diamonds Are Forever*.

With the disappearance of Blofeld from the Eon Series at the end of *Diamonds Are Forever*, the cat disappears also. However, during the pre-credits sequence of *For Your Eyes Only* the film-making give us a glimpse of Blofeld, and the cat makes a fleeting appearance, bringing its role – that of character identification – full circle.

PECK ON BOND: Film star and veteran performer Gregoy Peck once said of James Bond: 'He lives by an old showbusiness adage, give them a good show and always travel first class.'

PEGASUS: Max Zorin's (Christopher Walken) horse Pegasus wins at Ascot and by doing so alerts the secret service to Zorin's criminality in *A View To A Kill*. Bond and Tibbett (Patrick McNee) are working undercover at Zorin's stables and they discover the truth about Pegasus.

The horse has been fitted with a microchip and minute syringe in its leg. This allows Zorin to trigger an injection of natural steroids at a critical point in the race, giving Pegasus an extra advantage over competitors.

SHERIFF J. W. PEPPER: Louisiana State policeman, Sheriff J. W. Pepper (Clifton James), is a character providing comic relief in two consecutive Bond films. He first appears in *Live And Let Die* when 007 is chased through the Louisiana bayou by agents of Mr Big (Yaphet Kotto). Sheriff Pepper next runs into Bond in *The Man With The Golden Gun* while on holiday in Thailand.

PICTURE POSER: In a clever topical reference in the first film, *Dr No*, Eon Productions had a replica of the recently stolen Goya portrait of the Duke of Wellington on full display in *Dr No's* (Joseph Wiseman) private apartments. At the film's end, the Dr No complex is destroyed. But in *A View To A Kill*, made twenty-three years later, the picture appears in Max Zorin's (Christopher Walken) office at his stud farm near Paris.

PINEWOOD STUDIOS: Built in 1935 and opened in 1936 by millionaire Charles Boot, Pinewood Studios since *Dr No*, made in 1962, has been the traditional home for the making of the Bond series.

Filming of every 007 adventure has taken place at Pinewood, situated seventeen miles to the west of London. Among the more famous sets built there are those for Fort Knox in *Goldfinger* and the volcano-cum-rocket launching base in *You Only Live Twice*. The 007 stage burned down in 1984 but was rebuilt the same year.

The making of *Moonraker* during the winter of 1978 saw Pinewood used far less by Eon Productions. The production team had to move to studios in Paris. But even then, many of the effects sequences had to be shot at the British studios.

PISTE PROWESS: The cinematic Bond displays more than a passing proficiency on the ski slopes. Sean Connery's 007 is never seen ski-ing but George Lazenby has a stab at the activity. In *OHMSS* he features in two ski chases. Three of Roger Moore's films have a total of seven ski scenes. Associated with every ski scene has been John Glen, editor, second unit director and latterly director.

PLAY IT AGAIN: The same music often appears in more than one film. In *OHMSS*, three pieces from previous films, 'Under The Mango Tree' (*Dr No*), and the themes from *From Russia With Love* and *Thunderball*, are heard when 007 clears out his office after dictating his resignation.

Also in *OHMSS*, the theme from *Goldfinger* is heard at Marc-Ange Draco's (Gabriele Ferzetti) headquarters. A cleaner is whistling the tune.

A couple of bars from *Live And Let Die* is featured in *The Man With The Golden Gun*. This happens when Sheriff J. W. Pepper (Clifton James) sets eyes on Bond again. They first met in *Live And Let Die*.

And of course, consistently heard throughout the series is the James Bond Theme, featured in every film.

PLAYBOY CLUB: Bond is a member of the Playboy Club and Playboy Casino. His membership card is shown briefly in *Diamonds Are Forever*. The membership number is 40401.

POA: The secret visual display system featured at the nuclear submarine base at Faslane, Scotland in *The Spy Who Loved Me*, is a Polaris Operating Authority. In control is Captain Benson (George Baker). The POA computer can be used to show the last known location of British submarines. It can also be used to plot pre-arranged courses for submarines.

POISON: The British Secret Service, its allies and enemies, all use various kinds of poison. A minor employee of *Dr No* swallows cyanide rather than answer 007's questions. Agents of *Dr No* lace Bond's whisky with poison in his Jamaican hotel room.

Paula (Martine Beswick), Bond's helper in Nassau, takes poison to avoid being tortured by SPECTRE in *Thunderball*. SPECTRE agents in *From Russia With Love* wear shoes and boots with poison-tipped tongues of steel attached to the soles. This mechanism can be triggered at a moment's notice. During the film, Blofeld notes that it takes twelve seconds for a man to die by this process. The unfortunate victim is Kronsteen (Vladek Sheybal).

133

A sleeping Aki (Akiko Wakabayashi) is killed with poison in *You Only Live Twice*. The liquid is dropped into her mouth via a thin cord hanging from the ceiling. But 007 was the intended victim.

According to Bond in *Moonraker*, the ballpoint pen which conceals a poison-tipped needle – belonging to Holly Goodhead (Lois Chiles) is standard CIA equipment. It comes in handy when 007 is attacked by a huge snake at Hugo Drax's (Michael Lonsdale) hideaway in the South American jungle.

POISON PENS: Twice in the series, Bond has used pens which conceal more than ink in their barrels. In *Moonraker*, he purloins a standard issue CIA pen from Holly Goodhead (Lois Chiles). This pen contains a retractable poison-tipped needle. This saves Bond's life in a desperate life or death struggle with Hugo Drax's (Michael Lonsdale) pet python later in the film. 'Q' (Desmond Llewelyn) supplies Bond with an ordinary-looking fountain pen in *Octopussy*. But this contains a highly concentrated mixture of nitric and hydrochloric acid to dissolve metals. The pen top contains an ultra-sensitive listening device – compatible with the standard issues Secret Service bugging devices.

PRESIDENTIAL APPROVAL: Two US presidents have publicly stated an appreciation of James Bond, in both literary and cinematic form. President J. F. Kennedy claimed that he had read all the 007 books. When asked to compile a list of his ten favourite books he placed Fleming's *From Russia With Love* at number seven.

President Ronald Reagan paid tribute to Bond in Thames Television's special twenty-first birthday feature, *James Bond The First 21 Years*. President Reagan described the character as 'one of history's great heroes'. He added that Bond was skilled, witty, courageous and always got his girl. 'Bond is a man of honour – a symbol of real value in the world,' he stated.

President Reagan's former colleague in Government, General Alexander Haig, is also an admirer of Bond. He said on the television special that Bond 'kindled a spirit of adventurism'. General Haig added, 'I frequently wish in the anguish of diplomacy we could resort to this form of direct action which is one of his (Bond's) characteristic forms.'

PRINTOUT TRANSMISSION: Featured aboard the sub-marine-swallowing oil-tanker Liparus in *The Spy Who Loved Me*, printout transmission units are used to plot the position and intended movement of the two nuclear submarines used by Karl Stromberg (Curt Jurgens) in his planned destruction of New York and Moscow.

The positions of the submarines are:

Stromberg One –   39 degrees, 30–03 mins.
   firing at Moscow –   north
                         48 degrees, 00–0 mins. west.

Stromberg Two –   38 degrees, 17–1 mins.
   firing at New York –   north
                         22 degrees, 43–2 mins. west

The printout transmission units are used by Bond and Commander Carter (Shane Rimmer) of the US Navy to thwart Stromberg's plan. They take the position of the first submarine and pass it on to the second as a new target and vice versa so that the submarines destroy each other instead of the intended cities.

GROUP CAPTAIN PRITCHARD: A minor character in *Thunderball*, Group Captain Pritchard is played by Leonard Sachs, the long-time presenter of BBC Television's *Good Old Days* variety programme. Pritchard is the contact with whom Bond is ordered to liaise on Operation Thunderball.

PUSSFELLER: Owner of the seafront bar in *Dr No* is Pussfeller (Lester Prendergast). This is the bar where 007 meets Quarrel (John Kitzmiller) and Felix Leiter (Jack Lord). Pussfeller is reputed to be a strong man. When he grasps Bond from behind, Quarrel warns 007 that there is no use struggling because Pussfeller wrestles like an alligator. But 007 has little difficulty in throwing off his attacker.

Q-BRANCH: Equipment and gadgets from Q-Branch, the most secret of MI7's departments, are featured in all 007 films. 'Q' (Desmond Llewelyn), in all but two films, dispenses lifesaving devices vital in the work of 00 agents. Scenes from Q-Branch, situated deep below Whitehall, appear in four films: *Goldfinger, Diamonds Are Forever* (very briefly), *The Man With The Golden Gun* and *For Your Eyes Only*.

But Q-Branch has been seen to go 'on the road': Japan in *You Only Live Twice*, the Bahamas in *Thunderball*, Egypt in *The Spy Who Loved Me*, Brazil in *Moonraker* and India in *Octopussy*.

Q-CRAFT: Very much a water-borne version of the Aston Martin, the powerful Q-craft motor boat was furnished by Glastron Boat Company. The vessel is used by 007 in *Moonraker* on a trip to South America to investigate Drax's (Michael Lonsdale) activities. The Q-craft is equipped with mines, torpedoes and, for when Bond is chased to the edge of a daunting waterfall, an aerial escape route – a hidden hang-glider in the roof.

QUEEN OF CUPS: The Queen of Cups is one of the characters in the tarot cards sequence in *Live And Let Die*. The Queen of Cups in an upside down position is said to signify a deceitful and perverse woman. Just such a card is sent anonymously to Bond at his hotel in San Monique. This alerts 007 to the traitor Rosie Carver (Gloria Hendry), the CIA agent who doubles for Mr Big (Yaphet Kotto).

THE RACK: The traction device found in the Shrublands Health Farm in *Thunderball*. This is designed to stretch the spine. But SPECTRE agent Count Lippe (Guy Dolman) sabotages the machine when it is used by 007 – hoping that the British agent will be torn limb from limb.

RADIOACTIVE LINT: Apart from the combined safe cracking and photocopying machine used in Switzerland by Bond, the radioactive lint demonstrated by 'Q' (Desmond Llewelyn) at the beginning of *OHMSS* is the only product of Q-Branch to feature in the film.

'Q' believes that the benefits of radioactive lint are 'obvious' – placed in an opponent's pocket the lint can be tracked to provide a locational fix. This is a variation on the homing device principle used in *Goldfinger* and *The Man With The Golden Gun*.

RANGER DANGER: British nuclear submarine HMS Ranger, with sixteen Polaris missiles aboard, is hi-jacked by Karl Stromberg's (Curt Jurgens) submarine-stealing oil tanker in *The Spy Who Loved Me*. HMS Ranger's captain, Talbot (Bryan Marshall), dies during the fierce battle between Stromberg's men and a combined force of British, American and Soviet sailors who have been previously captured by the crew of the tanker Liparus.

REYNOLDS ON BOND: Movie star Burt Reynolds says of 007: 'We're very jealous of him in America.' But he adds, though incorrectly, 'he has not done a damn thing for America and we're pretty sick about it.'

TIM RICE: Lyricist and co-writer of such hits as 'Jesus Christ Superstar' and 'Evita', Tim Rice admits that writing the title song lyrics for *Octopussy* was among his more difficult jobs. Rice was sent John Barry's score and liked it. But he found it hard to write a romantic song around the title. In the end, he claims, he offered Bond producers eight titles and asked them to pick one. They chose 'All Time High' which was sung over the film's titles by Rita Coolidge.

HONEY RIDER: The first female lead in the series is Honey Rider (Ursula Andress). The first meeting between Bond and Honey on Crab Key is regarded by many as a classic scene of the British cinema. She emerges from the sea in a white bikini singing 'Under the Mango Tree'. According to Cubby Broccoli, Honey is every 'red-blooded male's fantasy'. Miss Andress is credited second in the cast list but her role is essentially a small one. The film is almost two thirds over before she makes an appearance and in the context of the plot everything could have happened without her presence.

RIGHT ROYAL: Her Majesty the Queen is referred to in *OHMSS*, *The Man With The Golden Gun*, *Octopussy* and *Moonraker*. In *Moonraker* it is announced, with much pride, that live television pictures of the victorious Bond and Holly Goodhead (Lois Chiles), beamed from *Moonraker 5*, are being transmitted directly to Buckingham Palace. Unfortunately, Her Majesty is treated to a weightless love scene between the couple.

ROLLS ROYCE: In a series featuring a plethora of rich and powerful men it comes as no surprise to learn that a classic status symbol of the wealthy, the Rolls Royce motor car, is a star in Bond movies on numerous occasions.

In *From Russia With Love*, Kerim Bey (Pedro Armendariz), 'M''s agent in Instanbul, owns a Rolls Royce and it is used to collect Bond from the airport. Kerim explains to 007 that the Rolls is useful when he wishes to make an unseen exit from the base. In the film he sends out dummies in the back of the car to fool enemy agents.

Draco (Gabriele Ferzetti), father of Tracy (Diana Rigg) and Bond's father-in-law in *OHMSS*, owns a light blue convertible Rolls – registration number 6640 TT75 with

French number plates – and it is in this car that Draco's men kidnap Bond to take the agent to his first meeting with Draco.

In *Moonraker*, Hugo Drax (Michael Lonsdale), like many other Bond villains, prefers a vintage Rolls – this time with Californian plates – and it is used to ferry Bond from the château to the pheasant shoot. Also in *Moonraker*, the British Secret Service in Rio de Janeiro collects Bond from the airport in a more modern Rolls – registration number NR 0002.

The villains in *For Your Eyes Only* and *Octopussy* – Kristatos (Julian Glover) and Kamal Khan (Louis Jourdan) respectively – own Rolls Royces. Kristatos possesses a white version, registration number E 667, for use in Corfu. While Kamal Khan goes for a vintage model with personalised plates, KAM 1.

Rolls Royce cars, beyond providing mere expensive toys for characters in the series, have also been used to further the action.

In *The Man With The Golden Gun*, Bond tails Scaramanga's (Christopher Lee) lover Andrea Anders (Maud Adams) in a green Rolls Royce registration number AU 603, and learns from Mary Goodnight (Britt Ekland) that all green Rolls Royces in Hong Kong are courtesy cars belonging to the Peninsula Hotel. This allows Bond to follow his quarry.

A View To A Kill has Bond, disguised as horse breeder James St John Smythe, and Sir Godfrey Tibbett (Patrick MacNee) disguised as his chauffer, arriving at Max Zorin's annual horse sales in a silver Rolls. It is in the same Rolls that an unconscious 007 and a dead Sir Godfrey are pushed into the middle of a deep lake by Zorin's (Christopher Walken) lover-bodyguard May Day (Grace Jones)

Perhaps the best example of a Rolls Royce providing part of the narrative structure comes in *Goldfinger*.

Like Hugo Drax and Prince Kamal Khan, Auric Goldfinger (Gert Frobe) prefers a vintage Rolls Royce, a gleaming version in yellow, a Phantom Three dating from 1937. With personalised plates, AU 1, the car is outstanding, but when Bond tracks it across the continent to Switzerland in his Aston Martin DB 5, he discovers the Rolls' secret – the bodywork and accessories are made of solid gold and this is the method by which Goldfinger smuggles gold out of England.

ROMANOFF STAR: The disappearance of the Romanoff Star, an historic national art treasure of the Soviet Union, leads to the downfall of General Orlov (Steven Berkoff), Bond's chief adversary in *Octopussy*. Orlov steals the star from the Kremlin Art Respository and substitutes it with a fake. But General Gogol (Walter Gotell) suspects that something underhand is going on.

TATIANA ROMANOVA: Tatiana 'my friends call me Tania', is SPECTRE's lure for Bond and she comes from Russia with love. Tatiana is a clerk working in the cipher department of the Soviet Embassy in Instanbul, we quickly learn in *From Russia With Love*. Her work is excellent and the state is proud of her – so says the splendidly wicked Rosa Klebb (Lotte Lenya), whose defection to SPECTRE from the KGB is unknown to Tatiana. Until she discovers the truth, she is 'doing it all for Mother Russia'. Tatiana is played by Italian actress Daniela Bianchi who gives a good account of herself in the role of a bright but basically naive agent.

ROOM SERVICE: Standard procedure for 007 when entering a hotel room is a search for bugging devices or hidden cameras. He goes through such routines in *Dr No*, *From Russia With Love*, *Thunderball*, *OHMSS*, *Live And Let Die*, *Octopussy* and *A View To A Kill*.

He also leaves little traps for uninvited guests while he is away from his room. In *Dr No*, Bond sprinkles talcum powder on his attaché case locks and positions a hair across the doors of his wardrobe. In *Thunderball*, he leaves a tape recorder hidden in a Bible to listen out for intruders. Q-Branch is a help in such matters, designing gadgets to trace hidden bugs, such as the one featured in *Live And Let Die* to check his hotel bungalow in the Caribbean. A later model, in the form of an electric shaver, is displayed in *A View To A Kill*.

ROYAL APPOINTMENT: The half-submerged wreck of the famous ocean-going liner the Queen Elizabeth I, which was left stricken in Hong Kong harbour in 1971, is used as an impromptu base for operations for the British in *The Man With The Goden Gun*. On board, 007 finds 'M' (Bernard Lee), 'Q' (Desmond Llewelyn) and Professor Frazier (Gerald James) who have all flown to Hong Kong on the operation to find the Solex Agitator – the essential unit to convert radiation from the sun into electricity on an industrial basis.

Bond is shown 'M''s room by a Royal Naval Officer. Along the way he sees the salvaging of a Chinese fighter aircraft and a bar populated with off-duty servicemen. 'With the Chinese on one side and the American fleet on the other, down here is the only place in Hong Kong where you can't be bugged,' quips the naval officer.

ROYAL COMMAND: *Daily Mail* gossip columnist Nigel Dempster reported in July 1986 that the most thumbed through books in the well-stocked library aboard the Royal Yacht Britannia are those in the complete set of James Bond adventures. The cinema aboard Britannia has also regularly shown 007 films. Most noticeably, the then recently released *For Your Eyes Only* was among the films requested by the Prince and Princess of Wales on their honeymoon in 1981.

RPM CONTROLLER: An electro-magnetic RPM controller is a small device worn on the little finger. It is demonstrated by 'Q' (Desmond Llewelyn) in a Las Vegas casino during *Diamonds Are Forever*. 'Q' explains to Tiffany Case (Jill St

John) that he has been aching to try it out. He proceeds to win the jackpot on every gaming machine he plays by using the device which causes the rotating cylinders to stutter and stop at a precise moment. Thus it ensures the winning symbol is displayed.

The significance of the electro-magnetic RPM controller is that it is one of the first gadgets to be employed simply for humour. Other examples include the remote controlled Indian rope trick in *Octopussy* and the umbrella that snaps shut like a Venus fly-trap in *For Your Eyes Only*.

RUNNING TIMES: As would be expected, running times in the series vary but most Bond movies average 120–130 minutes, about par for the course with most action films. The shortest 007 epic is *Dr No* which lasts 105 minutes and the longest is *OHMSS* which runs for 140 minutes.

SADDLE SCENES: Bond is seen riding a horse on five occasions. During his courtship with Tracy (Diana Rigg) in *OHMSS*, chasing a fleeing Beech 99 aircraft belonging to Kamal Khan (Louis Jourdan) in *Octopussy* and fighting a deadly duel with Max Zorin (Christopher Walken) in *A View To A Kill*. 007 also rides in *Moonraker* and *The Living Daylights*. Horse-riding villains are rare, numbering only three: the aforementioned Kamal Khan, Max Zorin and early Bondian adversary Auric Goldfinger (Gert Frobe), who, like Zorin, breeds thoroughbreds.

SADRUDDIN: Indian agent Sadruddin is employed by the British Secret Service in *Octopussy*. He is head of Station I in India. Sadruddin accompanies Bond on his first encounter with villain Prince Kamal Khan (Louis Jourdan). Sadruddin is played by Albert Moses, no stranger to the series. Moses played a barman in *The Spy Who Loved Me*.

SAFE-CRACKING DEVICES: On three occasions, 007 has

gained access to safes using equipment designed for that very purpose by Q-Branch.

Breaking into Osato Chemicals in *You Only Live Twice*, Bond has a pocket-sized safe-cracker, a box-shaped device with an extension which shows the combination numbers.

In the next film, *OHMSS*, Bond breaks into the safe belonging to Blofeld's lawyer, Gumbold, in Berne. This time he uses another safe-cracking device, much larger than the one used in the previous film, but this one also incorporates a photocopier.

The most compact device is displayed in *Moonraker*. Bond, investigating the activities of Hugo Drax, uses a safe-cracker housed in a cigarette case. This has X-ray capabilities and displays the inner workings of the safe.

SAKI: The traditional Japanese drink ordered by Bond in *You Only Live Twice*. Bond specifies that it should be served at the right temperature, 98.4 degrees Fahrenheit. Tiger Tanaka (Tetsuro Tamba), comments that for a European, Bond has a good knowledge of Japanese customs.

HARRY SALTZMAN: Canadian-born film producer Harry Saltzman co-produced nine Bond movies with Cubby Broccoli between 1962 and 1974. After the *The Man With The Golden Gun* his interest in the series waned and he sold out to United Artists.

Following the Second World War, Saltzman formed Woodfall Films with Tony Richardson and the duo went on to make cinema classics like *Look Back In Anger*, *The Entertainer* and *Saturday Night And Sunday Morning*. In the late 1950s the pair split up. Saltzman became interested in the Bond series of novels. He paid Fleming fifty thousand dollars for a six-month option on the books. But, surprisingly, he could not find a major film company interested in the project.

Saltzman learned that Cubby Broccoli was interested in a fifty-fifty deal and they became partners. Thus Eon

Productions was born and after a meeting with Arthur Krim, president of United Artists, in New York on June 20 1961, plans for the first film got off the ground.

BERT SAXBY: Casino manager at the Whyte House Hotel in *Diamonds Are Forever* is Bert Saxby (Bruce Cabot). Blofeld dispatches Saxby to murder the kidnapped Willard Whyte (Jimmy Dean) when it becomes obvious that Bond and the CIA are moving in on the diamond smuggling operation. But in his attempt to carry out this order, Saxby is shot by a CIA agent.

A sequence in Bert Saxby's office sees one of the series' in-jokes. A nameplate on the desk reads Albert R. Saxby – an unmistakable reference to Albert R. (Cubby) Broccoli.

Veteran actor Cabot appeared in the original *King Kong* movie.

SCARAMANGA: James Bond's chief adversary in *The Man With The Golden Gun* is played by Christopher Lee, of Dracula fame.

Scaramanga is from a circus family – his father was the ringmaster, possibly Cuban, and his mother was an English snake-charmer. He was a spectacular trick-shot artist by the time he was ten and a local Rio gunman at the age of fifteen. The KGB recruited him in Europe where, according to 007, he became an overworked, underpaid assassin. Scaramanga went independent in the late 1950s and by the 1970s his fee for a hit had soared to a million dollars.

Scaramanga confesses to Bond on their first meeting that his admitted love of killing derives from an experience he had as a child. In the circus his only real friend was a magnificent African bull elephant. Once, when the beast went berserk during training, the elephant's trainer emptied a gun into its eye. The young Scaramanga retaliated by emptying his stage pistol into the trainer's eye and thereby discovered his true vocation – 'You see Mr Bond, I always thought that I liked animals.

Then I discovered that I liked killing people even more.'

Scaramanga lives comfortably on a remote island off the Chinese coast. He pays no rent but in return for use of the island he does his oriental landlords 'the occasional favour'. As befits his title, Scaramanga displays a penchant for gold. He always uses a golden bullet – made by Lazar (Marne Maitland), a Portuguese gunsmith living in Macau – weighing 20.003 grammes and manufactured from soft 23 carat gold with traces of nickel. His unique golden gun allows complete freedom through airport X-ray machines since it can be broken down and appear as day-to-day accessories: a cigarette case, a pen, cuff-links and a lighter.

Scaramanga is tall, slim and dark. According to his mistress, Andrea Anders (Maud Adams), he always wears a white linen suit, a black tie and jewellery of gold. He also has one unmistakable feature – a third nipple. According to Hi-Fat (Richard Loo) some cults regard this as a sign of invulnerability and great sexual prowess. On that score, Scaramanga only ever makes love prior to a killing. He claims that it improves his eye.

Despite all his achievements, Scaramanga, like all great artists, wants to create one indisputable masterpiece in his lifetime and he believes that the death of James Bond in a face-to-face confrontation will be just that.

Christopher Lee, a distant cousin of Ian Fleming, was originally considered for the role of *Dr No*, but with Scaramanga Lee creates a truly memorable villain, a character whose deep-rooted malevolence is hidden by a surface coating of wit and charm.

SECRET SERVICE HQ: The location of the British Secret Service headquarters is not established in the series until *For Your Eyes Only*.

Up until then the Bond films tend to be coy in identifying the precise location of the building. Sometimes, as in *Dr No* and *Goldfinger*, we are given an establishing shot of the London skyline which then fades into an interior scene where Bond is given details of his latest mission.

With the advent of John Glen as director on the series, the location of the headquarters of MI7 has become much more definite. In *For Your Eyes Only*, the camera pans to an upper window of the Ministry of Defence – the inference being that this is where MI7 is based. Similar shots of the Ministry of Defence have been used as a prelude to Bond's briefing in *Octopussy* and *A View To A Kill* – both Glen-directed.

SHADY TREE: Nightclub entertainer Shady Tree (Leonard Barr) uses his comedy act which he claims he has not changed for forty years, as a cover for his involvement in diamond smuggling activities. He features in *Diamonds Are Forever*.

Shady Tree and his Acorns – two scantily dressed girls – perform in the Lincoln Lounge at Willard Whyte's (Jimmy Dean) Whyte House gambling house in Las Vegas. Shady is murdered by Blofeld's assassins Wint and Kid (Bruce Glover and Putter Smith).

SHARK GUN: A device used by Bond in *Live And Let Die* in the rescue of Solitaire (Jane Seymour) from the voodoo ceremony is a shark gun. The gun fires compressed gas pellets. This greatly amuses Mr Big (Yaphet Kotto) when he captures Bond, but the pellets are used by 007 to dispose of Mr Big. Bond forces a pellet into the mouth of his adversary and watches as the big man explodes like a over-inflated balloon.

SHARKS: Starring regularly in the Bond series are sharks. The first film to feature this creature that conveys a strong sense of menace is *Thunderball*. Emilio Largo (Adolfo Celi) collects big game fish for various marine institutions. He keeps a pool full of Golden Grotto sharks – 'the most savage, the most magnificent'.

Largo has a hidden tunnel connecting the shark pool to

a swimming pool. When Bond is discovered during a secret assault on Largo's Palmyra residence and falls into the pool while grappling with a SPECTRE agent, Largo opens a hatchway and lets the sharks into the swimming pool.

Mr Big (Yaphet Kotto), Bond's adversary in *Live And Let Die*, has a natural pool connected to the sea in his underground grotto. This is where the illicit supplies of heroin are processed. Cut off from the pool by means of a gate are a number of sharks. Mr Big cuts the arm of a trussed-up Bond and Solitaire (Jane Seymour) and allows the blood to drop into the water. He hopes this will encourage the sharks to eat the couple.

Karl Stromberg (Curt Jurgens) feeds erring employees and enemies to his sharks. His method of achieving this is particularly unpleasant. The floor of his elevator is hinged so that on the press of a button, victims drop in on the sharks. At the conclusion of *The Spy Who Loved Me*, Bond is successful in dropping Jaws (Richard Kiel), Stromberg's henchman, into the pool. But Jaws emerges unscathed after his encounter with the sharks.

Kristatos (Julian Glover) in *For Your Eyes Only* ties up Bond and Melina Havelock (Carole Bouquet) and drags them behind his yacht, across coral reefs, hoping that sharks will finish them off.

SHERRY: Bond is seen to drink a glass of sherry only once in the series. In *Diamonds Are Forever* he is served a glass of the fortified wine by Sir Donald Munger (Laurence Naismith). 007 correctly identifies the sherry as Solero, based on the original 1851 vintage.

SHOOT-OUT: During the gunfight scene at the gypsy encampment in *From Russia With Love*, Bond (Sean Connery) shoots eight people. John Barry's electric but haunting 007 Theme, used here rather than the James Bond Theme, makes it one of the most memorable scenes of the film.

SHRUBLANDS: The Shrublands Health Clinic situated near a NATO airbase in Sussex is the setting for much of the early action in *Thunderball*. It is here that Count Lippe (Guy Dolman), aided by SPECTRE's killer Fiona (Luciana Paluzzi) base their operation to swop the NATO observer aboard a Vulcan aircraft.

James Bond is sent to Shrublands presumably to recover from the wounds he received during the pre-credits sequence when he successfully managed to eliminate Colonel Jack Boiver at a château in France.

SILICON VALLEY: Heartland of the US electronics industry is Silicon Valley, California. The valley becomes the target for Max Zorin (Christopher Walken) in *A View To A Kill*. He is determined to destroy the area by an earthquake and flood, to establish a monopoly in the world microchip market. Silicon Valley has more than 250 specialised factories, employing thousands of scientists and technicians.

SILVER DATE: The twenty-fifth anniversary of the release of the first Bond film, *Dr No*, is on October 6th 1987. *Dr No* was premiered at the London Pavilion back in 1962.

BOB SIMMONS: Veteran stuntman Bob Simmons has been involved in the series since the beginning, and back in 1961 he was one of the original candidates for the 007 role. Simmons has contributed a variety of highly original fight sequences to the films.

Early on he doubled for Sean Connery. This is most noticeable in the tarantula sequence in *Dr No*. While in *Thunderball*, Simmons found himself wearing a dress and high heels while doubling as an actor playing a SPECTRE agent disguised as a woman.

Simmons doubled for Connery in the memorable fight aboard the Orient Express in *From Russia With Love* and he choreographed the stunning fight between Connery and Joe Robinson – playing Peter Franks – in the enclosed space of an elevator in *Diamonds Are Forever*.

SISTERS ROSE AND LILY: The fussy receptionists at Dr No's Crab Key complex, Sister Rose (Michele Mok) and Sister Lily (Yvonne Sima), are two of the series' more off-beat characters. The charming duo mother 007 and Honey (Ursula Andress) after they have been captured by Dr No's men.

SKY HIGH: Bond pilots a variety of aircraft. He attempts in *Goldfinger* to bring the recently-deceased Auric Goldfinger's (Gert Frobe) jet out of a steep dive after the sudden decompression of the fuselage. *Live And Let Die* sees 007 chased by gangsters loyal to Mr Big (Yaphet Kotto) to New Orleans' airport. Bond commandeers a Cessna training plane, complete with elderly American pupil, Mrs Bell (Ruth Kempf), and proceeds to elude his pursuers by roaring in between stationary planes and open hangars.

Bond gets airborne in a fixed-wing aircraft in *The Man With The Golden Gun* and *Octopussy*. In the former, 007 flies to Scaramanga's (Christopher Lee) island in Red Chinese waters in a small seaplane. In the pre-credits sequence of *Octopussy*, 007 escapes from an unnamed Latin American country in a tiny jet, the Acro-star. This is a plane small enough to hide in a horsebox.

In *You Only Live Twice*, Bond flies the famous Little Nellie autogyro. In the pre-credits sequence of *For Your Eyes Only* he takes control of a rogue helicopter sabotaged by Blofeld.

Bond eludes assailants in the pre-credits sequence of *Thunderball* by means of a jet pack strapped to his back. 007 flies a hang-glider twice. Once to gain access to Solitaire (Jane Seymour) at a remote Caribbean house in *Live And Let Die*, and again in *Moonraker* to avoid going over a South American waterfall in his Q-craft motorboat when chased by Jaws (Richard Kiel).

Five times 007 takes to parachutes: in *Goldfinger*,

Diamonds Are Forever, The Spy Who Loved Me, Moonraker and *The Living Daylights.*

MORTON SLUMBER: Proprietor of Slumber Incorporated, a crematorium in the Nevada desert, is the aptly-named Morton Slumber (David Bauer) – without doubt one of the series' blacker comical characters. Slumber features in *Diamonds Are Forever* in a sarcastic sideswipe by the scriptwriters at the commercial side of death.

Slumber is a link in the diamond smuggling pipeline. 007 comes close to death when he finds himself being roasted alive in Slumber's crematorium. But Bond lives to see another day.

PENELOPE SMALLBONE: Introduced to cinema audiences in *Octopussy* as a new assistant for Miss Moneypenny (Lois Maxwell), Miss Penelope Smallbone soon impresses 007. He presents her with a bouquet of flowers, originally intended for old flame Miss Moneypenny. Moneypenny advises Miss Smallbone: 'Take it, dear ... that's all you'll ever get from him.' Miss Smallbone is played by Michaela Clavell, daughter of novelist James Clavell.

SMITHERS: A character by the name of Smithers appears three times in the series. In *Goldfinger* we are introduced to Colonel Smithers, the governor of the Bank Of England, played by Richard Vernon. But in *For Your Eyes Only* and *Octopussy*, Smithers appears in a different guise played by Jeremy Bullock in both films. He is an aide to 'Q' (Desmond Llewelyn) and a secret service agent.

SMOKING: A fascinating reflection of changes in society over the course of the series is smoking. The literary character was a heavy smoker and had his cigarettes specially made for him by Morlands of Grosvenor Street, London. These customised cigarettes were a mixture of Balkan and Turkish tobacco with a much higher nicotine content than cheaper varieties. Fleming's Bond smoked sixty a day and got through seventy in an evening's gambling at Royale-les-Eaux.

In the early films Bond shares much the same habit. Indeed, Bond is first introduced lighting a cigarette at the beginning of *Dr No*. In *Dr No*, the only major character who does not smoke is Honey (Ursula Andress). Connery's Bond carries on smoking through the next four films. Only in the fifth film, *You Only Live Twice*, are references made, albeit mildly, to the dangers of Bond's habit.

George Lazenby's Bond smokes cigarettes in *OHMSS*. It is most noticeable in the pre-credits sequence when the new Bond is introduced, face unseen, lighting a cigarette in true Bondian fashion – shades of the Connery introduction. Lazenby is also seen to smoke a pipe – the only Bond that is seen to do so – when he travels to Blofeld's (Telly Savalas) lair disguised as Sir Hilary Bray.

But by 1971 with the release of *Diamonds Are Forever*, attitudes are changing. Bond does not smoke at all and in the following two films, *Live And Let Die* and *The Man With The Golden Gun*, he shows a preference for cigars. The subsequent Roger Moore films were marked by the fact that Bond does not smoke but Timothy Dalton's 007 smokes in *The Living Daylights*.

Other leading characters in the Bond series are hooked on the dreaded weed. 'M' (Bernard Lee) is famous for his pipe and Miss Moneypenny (Lois Maxwell) is seen smoking in her office during *From Russia With Love*.

Later films have featured the villains as the smokers. Although, in the early days, Emilio Largo (Adolfo Celi) in *Thunderball* used a lighted cigar for a more sinister purpose in torturing Domino (Claudine Auger). Blofeld (Telly Savalas and Charles Gray) smokes in *OHMSS* and *Diamonds Are Forever*.

In *From Russia With Love*, the film's two opposite views of womankind, the hideous Rosa Klebb (Lotte Lenya) and the beautiful Tatiana Romanova (Daniela Bianchi), are united in their smoking habits. Octopussy (Maud Adams) smokes during her first meeting with Bond. The advertising poster for *Dr No* shows Bond with a lighted cigarette in his left hand and the poster for *A View To A Kill* shows May Day (Grace Jones) standing back-to-back with Bond, casually lighting a cigarette in a long holder.

During the sail down the Nile to Cairo in *The Spy Who Loved Me*, Russia's Major Anya Amasova (Barbara Bach) knocks out Bond by blowing soporific gas at him from a phoney cigarette, while Bond uses a rocket in a cigarette in *You Only Live Twice* to dispose of one of Blofeld's (Donald Pleasence) guards at the volcano rocket base.

Live And Let Die sees Bond dispose of a poisonous snake planted in his bathroom by putting the lighted end of his cigar to an aerosol spray and burning the reptile to death in the resulting fire jet.

SNAKES: The first appearance of a snake is in *Live And Let Die*. British agent Baines (Dennis Edwards) is killed by snake venom at a voodoo ceremony. This happens during the pre-credits sequence. There is a near identical incident towards the end of the film. But Solitaire (Jane Seymour) does not share the same fate. Baron Samedi (Geoffrey Holder), an associate of Mr Big (Yaphet Kotto), is thrown by 007 into a coffin containing snakes during the rescue of Solitaire.

Bond is attacked by a snake in his bathroom later on in the feature.

007 is almost drowned by a giant python during *Moonraker*. He is thrown into a pool at Hugo Drax's (Michael Lonsdale) South American jungle hideaway. Bond survives by killing the beast with a poison-tipped needle secreted in a pen. 007 comments . . . 'he had a crush on me.'

While being chased by Kamal Khan (Louis Jourdan) and his men in *Octopussy* Bond finds himself sharing the Indian undergrowth with a snake. He tells the creature to 'hiss off'.

SNAP SHOT: A light-hearted but none the less handy device supplied to Bond by Q-branch in *Octopussy* is the crocodile suit that transforms into a tightly fitting personal submarine. This enables Bond to slip unnoticed between the shore and Octopussy's (Maud Adams) floating palace in India. The sight of the crocodile's mouth opening to reveal Roger Moore accompanied by suitable electronic sound effects inevitably evokes much mirth among the audience.

SNOW GO: Filming the Alpine action sequences of *For Your Eyes Only* in the Italian Dolomite mountains was hampered by an unseasonal lack of snow. The situation was remedied by the crew importing snow into the town of Cortina d' Ampezzo from another area of the mountains and shovelling it on to the streets.

SOLAR GUN: Featured in *The Man With The Golden Gun* is a solar gun. This device can focus on the energy generated from a solar power station into concentrated form for spectacularly destructive purposes. Scaramanga (Christopher Lee) demonstrates the power of the gun by blowing up Bond's sea plane. Remarking on the origin of the weapons energy, Scaramanga claims that he is truly 'the man with the golden gun'. The gun is a gift to the highest bidder for the design of the power station created and built by Hi-Fat Enterprises, of which Scaramanga is the chairman of the board.

SOLAR STATION: The secret at the heart of Scaramanga's (Christopher Lee) island off the coast of China in *The Man With The Golden Gun* is a solar energy station. The station – an enormously impressive set by production designer Peter Murton – is a vast complex containing thermo-electric generators which convert solar energy into electricity. The complex is fully automated, needing attention from only one extra opposed to the usual army of extras in other Bond films.

SOLEX AGITATOR: To convert radiation from the sun into electricity on an industrial basis, a solex agitator is an essential unit. It is featured in *The Man With The Golden Gun* It is claimed that the solex agitator is ninety-five per cent efficient enough to solve the world's energy problems. The device was developed by Gibson, the missing solar energy expert, for whom Bond is searching.

SOLITAIRE: Virginal mistress of the tarot cards, Solitaire (Jane Seymour) is the ward and virtual prisoner of Mr Big (Yaphet Kotto) in *Live And Let Die*. She harnesses her unique psychic powers for Mr Big's evil benefit. 007 makes love to Solitaire and this robs her of the ability to read tarot cards – thus ending her usefulness to Mr Big.

British actress Jane Seymour was chosen for the part after her success in the BBC television series *The Onedin Line*. Roger Moore, like Guy Hamilton, the director, and Tom Mankiewicz, the scriptwriter, thought that the character of Solitaire would have been much more interesting if she had been black. Mankiewicz had originally written the part for a black actress but United Artists, the distributors of the film, vetoed the idea.

SOUPER SHOW: British secret agent Campbell, based in Switzerland on 'M''s (Bernard Lee) orders, shadows Bond, disguised as Sir Hilary Bray, on his mission in *OHMSS* to infiltrate Blofeld's (Telly Savalas) Alpine headquarters. Campbell first helps 007 during the lunchtime assault on the offices of Blofeld's Berne lawyer, Gumbold (James Bree).

Campbell, a *Daily Express* reader and driver of a white Volkswagen Beetle, is an accomplished climber and follows 007 to Piz Gloria the hard way, up the side of a mountain.

Captured by SPECTRE, our last glimpse of the character sees him in the soup. Campbell is found frozen, upside down outside a window after Bond's cover is blown.

SPACE ACE: Bond is seen in a space suit on two occasions in the series. He almost makes it into space in *You Only Live Twice* when he assumes the identity of the SPECTRE astronaut at Blofeld's (Donald Pleasence) hidden rocket base in Japan. But 007 is captured before he can climb into the capsule. 007 makes it into orbit in *Moonraker*. He does this courtesy of Moonraker 6, one of the fleet of the space shuttles developed by Hugo Drax (Michael Lonsdale), piloted by NASA-trained Holly Goodhead (Lois Chiles).

SPACE STATION: Orbiting the Earth in *Moonraker* is a space station created by Hugo Drax (Michael Lonsdale). It was built by Drax Industries and is more than 200 metres in diameter and can accommodate a fleet of seven space shuttles at one time. The station is equipped with a radar jamming system which hides the station's position from Earth.

The station is central to Operation Orchid, Hugo Drax's plan to depopulate the planet. Phials containing nerve gas are to be launched from the station as a prelude to Operation Orchid. But at the conclusion of *Moonraker*, Drax's headquarters in the sky is destroyed when his forces are attacked by a crack squadron of US space paratroopers.

SPECTRE: The Special Executive for Counter-Intelligence, Terrorism, Revenge and Extortion is an organisation founded and headed by Ernst Stavro Blofeld and plays an integral part in every early film with the exception of *Goldfinger*.

The Roger Moore era has seen little mention of SPECTRE and Blofeld apart from a brief appearance of a Blofeld-style character – an unseen face stroking a white cat – in the pre-credits sequence of *For Your Eyes Only*.

SPECTRE employees, especially in the early films, all wear a standard uniform of black, tight-fitting clothes – emphasising the villainous nature of the organisation. The SPECTRE hierarchy is spared this particular discipline but sport the SPECTRE ring bearing the organisation's insignia – a design similar to a four-legged octopus.

The agents appear to be highly trained and we are given a glimpse of this in *From Russia With Love* when Rosa Klebb (Lotte Lenya) visits the SPECTRE base.

The organisation appears to have unlimited funds. Only in *You Only Live Twice* are financial backers mentioned. In this particular case it is Red China. To date, SPECTRE has lost hundreds of men and countless cars, boats, planes and spacecraft. Several bases have also gone the same way. Among the most notable are Dr No's complex, Blofeld's volcano hideaway and his mountain-top clinic and oil rig headquarters.

In *Thunderball*, SPECTRE headquarters is in Paris and operates a charitable front, the International Brotherhood for Stateless Persons.

SPECTRE ISLAND: Located somewhere in the Mediterranean, SPECTRE Island is the training headquarters for SPECTRE agents. We see a brief glimpse of the activities on the island in *From Russia With Love*. Rosa Klebb (Lotta Lenya) is escorted by Morzeny (Walter Gotell) to hit man Donald Grant (Robert Shaw). Morzeny is SPECTRE's training officer. This scene was filmed at Pinewood Studios.

SPIDER SHOCK: A spider placed inside Bond's bed by Professor Dent (Anthony Dawson) in *Dr No* is the first time that a creature is used to eliminate Bond. A similar scene appears in *Live And Let Die*. 007 is attacked in his bathroom by a snake.

SPIN SHOT: The sequence in *Dr No* when Bond and Miss Taro (Zena Marshall) make love is ended with a cut to a spinning fan. This device is often used by director Terence Young to emphasise love making. In *From Russia With Love*, he cuts away to the wheels of the Orient

Express, while in *Thunderball* the camera switches to the gyrating bodies of the Junkanoo procession.

SPIRAL JUMP: The scene in which Bond, in an American Motors Corporation Matador car, jumps over a river in Thailand to chase Scaramanga is one of the highlights of *The Man With The Golden Gun*. Bond completes a 360-degree spin with this mid-air spiral jump. The stunt was performed by W. J. Milligan Junior. The mathematical and computer technology used to calculate the stunt was furnished by Calspan Corporation of Buffalo, New York.

STAGE STRUCK: *The Spy Who Loved Me* saw the completion of the specially built 007 silent stage at Pinewood Studios in 1976. The stage, 374 feet in length, 160 feet in width and 35 feet high, was the world's largest sound stage. It was officially opened by former Prime Minister Harold Wilson. It accommodated the interior of the oil tanker Liparus which housed three nuclear submarines in the film. The stage was used by other leading film-makers, including the producers of the *Superman* series.

But on June 27th 1984 the stage was destroyed by fire during the shooting of *Legend*. By November the same year it was rebuilt and renamed the Albert R. Broccoli 007 Stage in time for the filming of *A View To A Kill*.

STEAMING AHEAD: The Nene Valley International Steam Railway, near Peterborough, Cambridgeshire, was taken over by Eon Productions in September 1982 for the filming of *Octopussy*. The line and rolling stock doubled for the scenes when the Octopussy circus travels by train between East and West Germany. Wansford Station was converted to represent Karl Marx Stadt. The locomotive, No. 73050, which usually pulls carriages of tourists around the steam railway, became an East German locomotive.

The train featured in *Octopussy* was driven by Prince Edward in June 1986 at the opening of an extension to the Nene Valley Railway.

STEPPING OUT: Only once in the series is Bond seen dancing. This happens in *Thunderball* when Sean Connery takes to the floor twice.

In the first sequence, Bond dances with Domino Derval (Claudine Auger) during his determined seduction of her which he hopes will uncover more about her 'guardian' Emilio Largo (Adolfo Celi). Domino is clearly impressed by Bond's technique, 'especially the way you hold me'.

The second sequence sees Bond, chased and wounded during the Junkanoo procession. He dashes into the Kiss Kiss night club to avert attention. He grabs a girl and leads her to the dance floor. However, Fiona (Luciana Paluzzi) sees him and splits the couple. During his enforced dance with Fiona, Bond confides: 'I enjoy my dancing'.

STRANGWAYS: Tim Moxon plays Strangways, the Jamaica-based British Secret Service agent in *Dr No*. Strangways and his secretary (Dolores Keator) are murdered, and this leads to Bond's first screen mission.

KARL STROMBERG: 'Why do we seek to conquer space when seven-tenths of our universe remains to be explored?' With these words Karl Stromberg (Curt Jurgens) reveals his passion for the sea, a passion that develops into a mania for destruction of the land-based population by the use of stolen nuclear weapons. Stromberg wants to start a human colony on the sea bed.

Stromberg lives as a recluse in his marine laboratory on the seabed off Sardinia. Surrounded by a vast array of marine life he wants for nothing else. He is head of the Stromberg Shipping Line of which the huge Liparus oil tanker is his pride and joy. The tanker is used to steal submarines.

Like many Bond villains, Stromberg has a physical deformity. He has webbed fingers and is loathe to shake hands with people. Stromberg is killed at the end of *The Spy Who Loved Me* by four bullets from Bond's Walther PPK.

HAROLD STRUTTER: CIA agent Harold Strutter (Lon Sutton) comes to Bond's rescue in *Live And Let Die*. 007 is in New York's Harlem district on the trail of Mr Big (Yaphet Kotto). Mr Big orders that Bond should be 'wasted' but Strutter is on hand to save the day for the British agent. Strutter makes a wry remark about Bond's lack of disguise: 'White face in Harlem – good thinking Bond.'

Strutter is murdered by agents of Mr Big while keeping an eye on the Fillet of Soul restaurant in Docker Street, New Orleans.

SUB-TITLES: The series uses sub-titles sparingly and then only to identify a particular location. The most frequent use of sub-titles occurs in the pre-credits sequence of *Live And Let Die* when the three changes of location – New York, New Orleans and San Monique – are accompanied by sub-titles.

SUMO WRESTLERS: Afforded the rank of superstars in Japan, these huge, almost grotesque figures, have featured in two Bond films. *You Only Live Twice* sees Bond meeting Aki (Akiko Wakabayashi), his contact with the Japanese Secret Service, at a Sumo wrestling match in Tokyo. Later in the film British agent Henderson (Charles Gray) is murdered by a man built like a Sumo wrestler who throws Bond as if he is a rag doll during a fight at Osato Chemicals.

The Man With The Golden Gun features 007 attacked by two Sumo wrestlers at night in Hi Fat's (Richard Loo) garden.

SUNGLASSES: Surprisingly for such a cool character, Bond wears sunglasses only four times during the series. In *From Russia With Love* he wears a pair to effect a disguise as he makes a hazardous rendezvous with Tatiana Romanova (Daniela Bianchi) on a ferry off the coast of Turkey. *Thunderball* sees our hero slip on a pair of sunglasses to hide the hardness in his eyes when telling Domino (Claudine Auger) of the death of her brother

François and to request help to defeat Emilio Largo (Adolfo Celi).

007 briefly wears a pair of sunglasses in the pre-credits sequence of *OHMSS* when driving the famous Aston Martin. 'Q' (Desmond Llewelyn) supplies Bond with a special pair in *A View To A Kill* which are fitted with infra-red filters, operated by a tiny lever, to enable the agent to see inside a darkened room.

SUPERMAC: Former Beatle Paul McCartney and his wife Linda composed the theme song for *Live And Let Die*. The score was nominated for an Academy Award for best original song in 1973.

STACEY SUTTON: Taking the leading female role in *A View To A Kill* is Stacey Sutton (Tanya Roberts). Stacey is a fully qualified geologist who works for California's Department of Conservation at City Hall, San Francisco. As a child, Stacey was expected eventually to take over the reins of the family firm, Sutton Oil, founded by her grandfather. At college she studied geology. But Max Zorin (Christopher Walken) stood in her way, taking over Sutton Oil.

Stacey has tackled Zorin in the courts but the cost has been high. She has been forced to sell her furniture. By taking a job at the City Hall she has been able to hold on to the house – built by her grandfather – and her shares. At the time that Bond enters her life, Zorin has offered Stacey five million dollars for her shares. This is ten times more than they are worth. Zorin is attempting to persuade Stacey to drop a law suit against him and leave his way clear to instigate Project Mainstrike.

KISSY SUZUKI: Japanese agent Kissy Suzuki (Mie Hama) in *You Only Live Twice* lives on the fishing island of Ama off the coast of Japan. She works for Tiger Tanaka (Tetsuro Tamba) of the Japanese SIS: Kissy 'marries' 007 – disguised as a poor fisherman – as a prelude to the attack on Blofeld's volcano headquarters. But the ceremony is null and void as Bond gives a false name to the priest.

TIGER TANAKA: *You Only Live Twice* introduces Tiger Tanaka (Tetsuro Tamba). Cheerful head of Japanese SIS, Tanaka is in charge of a force of highly-trained Ninja warriors – experts in the ancient arts of concealment. Tanaka has an underground railway to travel around Tokyo. He explains to Bond that his job makes it unwise for him to rely on more conventional methods.

MISS TARO: The first of a long line of female villains, Miss Taro (Zena Marshall) is an agent for *Dr No*, planted as a secretary at Government House in Jamaica.

Miss Taro invites Bond to join her at their bungalow in the mountains. This is a trap. She plots that 007 should be murdered en route. But the attempt on Bond's life fails. Miss Taro is arrested.

TAROT CARDS: Throughout *Live And Let Die*, the visual presence of tarot cards is used most effectively in publicising the feature. Solitaire (Jane Seymour) reads tarot cards for Kananga/Mr Big (Yaphet Kotto). By this means, Solitaire is able to follow Bond's journey from England to New York and also predict his movements.

The cards suggest that 007 and Solitaire are destined to become lovers. But it is the consummation of this love that robs Solitaire of her ability to read the cards. Bond visits Solitaire by arriving courtesy of a hang-glider.

The tarot cards for the film were designed by Fergus Hall.

TEE-HEE: Henchman for Mr Big (Yaphet Kotto) in *Live And Let Die*. Tee-Hee (Julius W. Harris) is a chuckling villain – hence the name – with a grip of steel and a clear penchant for sadism. Played by gentle actor Harris – one of Roger Moore's friends on the set, Tee-Hee is one of the series' more memorable characters.

He is equipped with a metal arm to replace the limb he lost to a crocodile's teeth in a careless moment. Tee-Hee's best scene comes when leaving Bond alone on a bed-sized island in the midst of a crocodile pool. His cruel laugh underlines the serious nature of Bond's predicament.

Harris, who in real life has a full complement of limbs, had his right arm strapped to one side during the filming. This made room for the metal arm which was controlled by his breathing. Initially, this process left the actor in some difficulty.

SIR GODFREY TIBBETT: Secret service agent masquerading as a racehorse trainer in *A View To A Kill*, Sir Godfrey Tibbett (Patrick MacNee) is introduced to Bond at Ascot races. Later in the film when 007 poses as horse breeder James St John Smythe, Tibbett takes on the role of his chauffeur. However, Tibbett is murdered in a French car wash by Max Zorin's (Christopher Walken) bodyguard, May Day (Grace Jones).

TIME SPAN: The longest period of time covered by the narrative of a Bond film is four months in *OHMSS*. The film opens in the first couple of weeks of September and ends after the following Christmas. This was a testing assignment for 007 who also found and lost a wife during this period.

The shortest span is probably in *Dr No*. The action takes place over a matter of a few days.

TIMING: Wristwatches provide the basis for many a splendid gadget. In *From Russia With Love*, SPECTRE hit man Donald Grant (Robert Shaw) is equipped with a nasty accessory to his timepiece. A strand of wire extends from the winding button and this can be used to garrot enemies.

'Q' (Desmond Llewelyn) supplies Bond with a wrist-watch fitted with a geiger counter in *Thunderball*. Handy for tracking down the whereabouts of missing nuclear devices. While in *Live And Let Die*, 007 is presented with a watch equipped with a magnetic field able to deflect the path of bullets. The gadget also contains a tiny saw on the outer rim. This comes to Bond's and Solitaire's rescue at the climax of the picture.

In *The Spy Who Loved Me*, Bond's watch is fitted with a radio receiving device to keep him in direct contact with 'M' (Bernard Lee). In the pre-credits sequence his watch receives ticker-tape messages.

This array of amazing timepieces continues in *Moonraker*. His wristwatch has a small supply of explosives and 007 is able to blast himself out of the confines of prison. In *For Your Eyes Only* the secret agent's watch once more has a direct link with headquarters. This plays a part in the humorous end when Mrs Thatcher finds herself speaking to a parrot via the device.

Octopussy sees 'Q' (Desmond Llewelyn) equipping Bond with a watch fitted with a receiver able to pick up the signals of a homing device.

TITLE CHANGES: Title changes are rare in the Bond series but they have occurred.

At the end of *The Spy Who Loved Me*, it is announced that, 'James Bond will return in *For Your Eyes Only*,' but the title of the next film was changed to *Moonraker*, with *For Your Eyes Only* being the next production. Thus, *For Your Eyes Only* has been announced as the next Eon Production at the end of two films – *The Spy Who Loved Me* and *Moonraker* – the only time that this has occurred in the series.

The end credits of *Octopussy* stated that the next film was to be *From A View To A Kill*, but the title of the next feature is *A View To A Kill*, the 'From' having been dropped. *From A View To A Kill* is actually a Fleming title.

No title is given at the end of *A View To A Kill* as being the next production – another departure from set formula – but the announcement early in 1986 that the next Bond film would be entitled *The Living Daylights* was postponed at the last moment when MGM/UA became unsure of its effectiveness as a title. *The Living Daylights* is a Fleming title and will enjoy the distinction of being the film to celebrate twenty-five years of James Bond in the cinema.

TOPPLING: The use of radio beams to destroy the gyroscopic controls of a guided missile or spacecraft. This method of destruction was used by Dr No (Joseph Wiseman) to interfere with American rockets launched from Cape Canaveral.

TRACKING SYSTEM: Mega-villain Karl Stromberg (Curt Jurgens) uses an ingenious tracking system to steal submarines in *The Spy Who Loved Me*. Heat signature recognition allows the satellite to pinpoint a submerged submarine by its wake and in turn leads Stromberg to his quarry. The British secret service and the KGB are alerted to Stromberg's activities when the system is offered for sale by a treacherous employee of Stromberg, Felicca (Olga Bisera).

TRAINING GROUND: The SPECTRE training ground in *From Russia With Love* is in reality the grounds of Pinewood Studios, Buckinghamshire, England. The parachute finale of *Goldfinger* used the same location and, indeed, careful viewing of the two sequences can identify the same trees.

TRIANA: We are introduced to Sir Timothy Havelock (Jack Hedley) and his ship the Triana in *For Your Eyes Only*. The Triana operates not only as a floating home for marine biologist Sir Timothy and his wife Iona (Toby Robins) but also as Sir Timothy's exploration and salvaging vessel. The Triana is equipped with Neptune, a two-man submarine especially designed for salvage work.

It is while they are aboard the Triana that Sir Timothy and his wife are murdered by Hector Gozales (Stefan

Kalipha), a Cuban hit man working for Kristatos (Julian Glover).

TURKISH DELIGHT: The Turkish Ministry of Information gave consent for Eon Productions to film scenes for *From Russia With Love* within the Saint Sophia Mosque in Istanbul. This was allowed providing that filming did not interrupt life inside the ancient building. Thus, the moody sequence inside Saint Sophia which appears in the film features real tourists in the background rather than extras.

UNDERWATER ANTICS: Underwater sequences have featured in seven films of the series but the most extensive were in *Thunderball* of which the action sequences and special effects beneath the waves were the highlight. Under the direction of Ricou Browning these pleasing scenes were shot by the Ivan Tors Underwater Studios. Underwater cameraman Lamar Boren and engineer Jordan Klein must take much of the credit, too.

The climax of the film is an exciting battle between Bond with a troop of US aqua-paratroopers and the SPECTRE forces possessing the nuclear weapons.

The Spy Who Loved Me sees Bond and Anya Amasova (Barbara Bach) tackling the forces of Karl Stromberg (Curt Jurgens) beneath the seas off the coast of Sardinia in 007's submarine-convertible Lotus Esprit car. In *Goldfinger*, Bond wears a wetsuit which masks an elegant white dinner jacket. Bond is also seen to wear a wetsuit in *Thunderball, You Only Live Twice, For Your Eyes Only* and *A View To A Kill*.

Other underwater sequences feature in *You Only Live Twice, Live And Let Die, Moonraker* and *A View To A Kill*.

UNIFORM APPEARANCE: As a Royal Navy commander, 007 is seen to wear a Naval uniform twice in the series. Bond is buried at sea in full uniform – as befitting an officer of the navy – in *You Only Live Twice*. His 'murder' has been staged to fool his enemies into believing he is dead.

The Spy Who Loved Me has much lengthier sequences with Bond in uniform. When first assigned to the missing submarine case, Bond meets with the Minister of Defence, Frederick Gray (Geoffrey Keen) at a Scottish submarine base. Bond wears a Naval uniform when joining the American submarine USS Wayne to shadow Karl Stromberg's (Curt Jurgens) vessel, the Liparus. He remains in uniform for the rest of the film.

Bond also appears in uniform in the pre-credits sequence of *Octopussy* – that of a Colonel in the army of the unnamed South American country whose aircraft 007 is attempting to sabotage.

UNION CORSE: The cinema is introduced to Union Corse, a Mafia-style organisation headed by Marc-Ange Draco (Gabriele Ferzetti), in *OHMSS*. Marc-Ange Draco is the father of Tracy (Diana Rigg) – the ill-fated Mrs Bond.

At the first meeting between Bond and Draco, 007 is told that Union Corse is the biggest criminal organisation in Europe. But Bond corrects him by reminding Draco that SPECTRE is larger because it operates worldwide.

Although strictly a criminal organisation, Union Corse proves to be of enormous help to Bond. Draco and his men join with Bond in their dual mission of rescuing Tracy from Blofeld and destroying the Piz Gloria clinic in Switzerland.

The criminal nature of the organisation is ignored by 'M' (Bernard Lee), 'Q' (Desmond Llewelyn) and Miss Moneypenny (Lois Maxwell). They quite happily stand alongside Draco's men at the wedding of Bond and Tracy.

Indeed, 'M' is displayed as having high regard for Draco. At one stage 'M' congratulates Draco on the 1964 'bullion job', when we learn Draco's men got away with a large haul of gold.

UPS AND DOWNS: Lifts, or elevators as they are known in the US, feature extensively in the series and often form an integral part of an action sequence. One of the most memorable scenes is in *A View To A Kill* when Max Zorin (Christopher Walken) ensnares Bond and Stacey Sutton (Tanya Roberts) in a lift between floors. Zorin throws a petrol bomb down the shaft. Karl Stromberg (Curt Jurgens) in *The Spy Who Loved Me* has lifts fitted with trap doors at his Atlantis stronghold. Enemy agents and erring employees can be delivered down the lift shaft into a shark-infested pool.

Blofeld (Charles Gray) in *Diamonds Are Forever* has a lift equipped with knock-out gas in his Las Vegas penthouse. The film also features the splendid fight between Bond and Peter Franks (Joe Robinson) in an Amsterdam lift.

VAVRA: Leader of the gypsies in *From Russia With Love* is Vavra. Bond and Kerim Bey (Pedro Armendariz) visit a gypsy camp to elude Eastern-Bloc agents. 007 saves Vavra's life in a gunfight and the gypsy leader proclaims that Bond is now one of his sons.

VENINI GLASS: The Venini Glass shop a few yards away from St Mark's square in Venice was used as a location in *Moonraker*. It is said to be a subsidiary of Drax Industries, which, when investigated by 007, is found to be the plant where glass phials are made to contain nerve gas intended for use in Operation Orchid. This is part of Hugo Drax's (Michael Lonsdale) plan to depopulate the world.

VIDA: Played by Aliza Gar, Vida is a participant in the gypsy girl brawl in *From Russia With Love*. This is a prelude to the gun battle beween Bond and his allies and the Eastern Bloc agents at the gypsy camp.

VIRUS OMEGA: Blofeld (Telly Savalas) develops Virus Omega at his alpine clinic, Piz Gloria, in *OHMSS*. The virus is the weapon intended for use in Blofeld's bacteriological assault on world crops and livestock.

Virus Omega is far more lethal than any other bacteriological agent ever before developed, Blofeld boasts to Bond. The virus has the capacity to induce sterility in complete strains of crops and animals.

FIONA VOLPE: With flaming red hair, deceptive femininity and a rocket-firing motor-cycle, Fiona Volpe (Luciana Paluzzi) is a SPECTRE executioner in *Thunderball*. Fiona has been described as having a blood-thirsty sexuality. It is this aspect of the Italian Miss Paluzzi's performance that makes the character so convincing. Bond discovers that Fiona is a fast lady when she takes him for a ride in her blue Mustang sports car. An expert shot, she proves to be ruthless in her work. Bond discovers that she makes love like a wild animal. But Fiona can also play the graceful lady. The true nature of her activities is apparent to 007 when he discovers she is wearing a SPECTRE ring.

VOODOO SHOP: New York gangster Mr Big (Yaphet Kotto), Bond's adversary in *Live And Let Die*, uses the Oh Cult Voodoo Shop as a cover for his evil activities. The shop – the assistant is played by Kubi Chaza – sells a bizarre range of goods, including skulls which are sold for sacrifices, but its main function is to provide a front for the garaging of Mr Big's fleet of cars.

KEN WALLIS: Wing Commander Ken Wallis, the inventor of Little Nellie, the autogyro star of *You Only Live Twice*, is the holder of sixteen autogyro world records. Wing Commander Wallis has a collection of fourteen autogyros at his Norfolk home and in 1982 took the aircraft to a record 18,253 feet over Boscombe Down, Wiltshire. In 1974 he received the Breguet Trophy from Prince Philip for his achievements in aviation.

WALTHER PPK: Bond is first acquainted with his Walther PPK handgun in *Dr No*. In this sequence, Bond has just returned from six months' sick leave as a result of his previous weapon, a Beretta, jamming on him (we are not told what the circumstances are). Bond is then issued with his famous Walther.

The Walther PPK was standard issue with the British Secret Service until 1974 when it was withdrawn from service. It is believed that this decision was taken following an incident in the Mall, near Buckingham Palace, when there was an attempt to kidnap Princess Anne. The gun jammed when it was being used by a Royal bodyguard and was withdrawn from use. In the series, though, Bond continues to use the Walther PPK.

Moonraker is the only film in which our hero is never seen with his Walther. He uses a shotgun but is not seen to carry a personal weapon.

WEDDINGS: Apart from James Bond's wedding to Tracy (Diana Rigg) in *OHMSS*, a ceremony attended by 'M' (Bernard Lee), 'Q' (Desmond Llewelyn) and Miss Moneypenny (Lois Maxwell), the series has featured four other weddings, most of which have provided an amusing background to the central action of the film.

Bond poses as a poor fisherman in *You Only Live Twice*, and takes part in a traditional Japanese wedding ceremony with Kissy Suzuki (Mie Hama), an agent of Tiger Tanaka (Tetsuro Tamba), to further effect his disguise. Bond gives a false name to the priest, making the marriage null and void. Kissy coyly reminds him of this, disqualifying any ideas he might have had of a honeymoon.

Bond's speedboat escape from Mr Big's (Yaphet Kotto) Louisiana crocodile farm in *Live And Let Die* interrupts a lakeside wedding ceremony.

Towards the end of *For Your Eyes Only*, Bond meets 'Q' disguised as a Greek priest in a tiny Greek village to receive information regarding Kristatos (Julian Glover). While they meet in a church the village is out celebrating a wedding.

Pursuing May Day (Grace Jones) through the streets of Paris in *A View To A Kill*, Bond crashes through the glass top of a pleasure boat on the River Seine in which a wedding reception is underway. Bond lands on top of the wedding cake and, before leaving, pauses to hand the unhappy couple the only tier of the cake to survive his fall.

WET-BIKE: A gimmicky cross between a speedboat and a motor-cycle adds yet another dimension of fun to water sport in *The Spy Who Loved Me*. A wet-bike is sent to Bond aboard the USS Wayne submarine from Q-branch in a diplomatic bag. The machine is used by 007 to cover the distance between the submarine and Karl Stromberg's (Curt Jurgens) Atlantis for the final dual between the British agent and the criminal mastermind.

The wet-bike was furnished by Artic Enterprises of Thief River Falls, Minnesota.

WHISPER: A heavily built character in *Live And Let Die* in the employ of Mr Big (Yaphet Kotto), Whisper (Earl Jolly Brown) weighed nearly three hundred pounds at the time of filming.

MRS WHISTLER: Innocuous-looking Mrs Whistler (Margaret Lacey) features in *Diamonds Are Forever* as a teacher in South Africa. But a darker side is revealed when we discover she is a courier for a diamond smuggling syndicate. Gems are transported from Africa to Tiffany Case (Jill St John) in Amsterdam. Mrs Whistler is murdered by Wint and Kidd (Bruce Glover and Putter Smith). She drowns in an Amsterdam canal.

WILLARD WHYTE: Mysterious billionaire Willard Whyte (Jimmy Dean) is a central character in *Diamonds Are Forever*. Whyte is a recluse of the Howard Hughes vogue and lives in a penthouse suite at the Whyte House in Las Vegas. We are told that Whyte has not set foot outside his home in five years.

Bond visits the Whyte House to discover for himself what lies behind the mystery. 007 finds that Whyte has been kidnapped by Blofeld (Charles Gray). Whyte's empire is vast, embracing oil, electronics, building, aviation and arms. Whyte Tectronics undertakes US Government contracts. Among the work being carried out is a project to build a moon buggy.

MICHAEL G. WILSON: Born in New York, the stepson of Cubby Broccoli, Michael Wilson graduated from college as an electrical engineer before studying law at Stanford University. He joined Eon Productions in 1972 as a legal administrator. In 1977 he was named as assistant to the producer on *The Spy Who Loved Me*.

Wilson became executive producer on *Moonraker* and fulfilled the same role on *For Your Eyes Only* and *Octopussy*. He was then elevated to co-produce with Broccoli on *A View To A Kill*.

Away from the world of film production, Wilson is an excellent photographer – and a leading expert on early English photographs – an accomplished skier and a proficient scuba diver.

He has also contributed in the role of a scriptwriter. Co-writing with Richard Maibaum, he helped produce the scripts for *For Your Eyes Only*, *Octopussy*, *A View To A Kill* and *The Living Daylights*.

WINT AND KIDD: Homosexual partners in crime, Mr Wint and Mr Kidd are henchmen employed by Blofeld (Charles Gray) in *Diamonds Are Forever*. Wint (Bruce Glover) and Kidd (Putter Smith) seem to savour each killing and puns abound in the script as they perform their work. 'Heart warming, Mr Wint', 'a glowing tribute, Mr Kidd', are their comments as attempts are made to roast 007 alive in Morton Slumber's (David Bauer) crematorium.

But Wint and Kidd meet an explosive end. Their plan to kill Bond on the Canberra goes wrong and 007 burns Mr Kidd alive – revenge, perhaps, for the earlier attempt – and despatches Wint over the side of the ship with a bomb clipped to his coat tails.

WOMAN TROUBLES: Surprisingly for such a gentleman, Bond has resorted to force and struck the fairer sex on four occasions in front of the camera. The most savage slap is the one he gives to a startled Tatiana Romanova (Daniela Bianchi) in *From Russia With Love*. This happens aboard the Orient Express when 007 discovers the death of his ally Kerim Bey (Pedro Armendariz) and believes that Tatiana is somehow implicated.

Bond slaps Tracy (Diana Rigg), his future wife in *OHMSS*. She pulls a gun on him in his hotel room. She wonders aloud whether she should kill 007 'for a thrill'. Tiffany Case (Jill St John) gets a smack from Bond in *Diamonds Are Forever* after she becomes difficult in the face of his questions.

But it is Andrea Anders (Maud Adams), girlfriend of Scaramanga (Christopher Lee) in *The Man With The Golden Gun*, who comes off the worst. She receives an uncharacteristic beating up from Bond when she attempts to evade his questions regarding her lover and supply of golden bullets.

The pre-credits sequence of *Thunderball* purports to show Bond punching a woman on the chin. But the 'woman' turns out to be a male enemy agent in disguise.

Perhaps the most vicious attack on a woman is at the hands of Mr Big (Yaphet Kotto). He discovers that Solitaire (Jane Seymour) has slept with Bond. Mr Big strikes Solitaire so hard that she is flung to the ground in this scene from *Live And Let Die*.

CHRISTOPHER WOOD: British screenwriter Christopher Wood co-wrote *The Spy Who Loved Me* with Richard Maibaum. He received a solo screenplay credit for *Moonraker*. Wood also penned two paperback novelisations of scripts on which he worked.

WRIST TWIST: *Moonraker* sees Q-branch supply Bond with a wrist gun. It is strapped to his right wrist and hidden under the sleeve. The gun comes supplied with ten darts.

Five are red-tipped and cyanide-coated to cause death within thirty seconds and the others have armour-piercing heads.

Bond uses the device twice in *Moonraker* to sabotage the centrifuge trainer in which Hugo Drax's (Michael Lonsdale) accomplice Chang is attempting to kill him and later, at the film's conclusion, to kill Drax aboard his space station.

WRITE ON: Bond films have credited only ten scriptwriters on the fourteen Eon-produced pictures – no mean achievement over twenty-five years. The major contributing writer is veteran Richard Maibaum. He has written or co-written *Dr No, From Russia With Love, Goldfinger, Thunderball, OHMSS, Diamonds Are Forever, The Man With The Golden Gun, The Spy Who Loved Me, For Your Eyes Only, Octopussy, A View To A Kill* and *The Living Daylights*.

In addition, Joanna Harwood and Berkely Mather co-wrote *Dr No*, Joanna Harwood co-wrote *From Russia With Love*, Paul Dehn co-wrote *Goldfinger*, John Hopkins co-wrote *Thunderball*, Roald Dahl wrote *You Only Live Twice*, Tom Mankiewicz co-wrote *Live And Let Die*, Christopher Wood co-wrote *The Spy Who Loved Me* and wrote *Moonraker*, George McDonald Fraser co-wrote *Octopussy*, Michael G. Wilson co-wrote *For Your Eyes Only, Octopussy, A View To A Kill* and *The Living Daylights*.

YES MINISTER: Bondian adventures come into contact with a procession of Government ministers. The outset of *The Spy Who Loved Me* sees 'M' (Bernard Lee) speaking on the telephone to the Prime Minister. The splendidly offbeat conclusion to *For Your Eyes Only* has Prime Minister Margaret Thatcher and husband Denis – played by Janet Brown and John Wells – in some difficulty over contacting 007. The Prime Minister is also mentioned in *Thunderball, OHMSS* and *The Man With The Golden Gun*.

Thunderball features the Home Secretary, played by Roland Culver. The end credits identify the role, incorrectly, as the Foreign Secretary. A fictional Minister of Defence, Frederick Gray, features in *The Spy Who Loved Me*, *Moonraker*, *For Your Eyes Only*, *Octopussy* and *A View To A Kill*, played by Geoffrey Keen.

YO-YO SAW: Indian thug (William Derrick) uses a fearsome device, two circular saws brandished in the same manner as a child would play with a yo-yo, to murder Bond's helper in *Octopussy*, Vijay (Vijay Amritraj). This hit man is in the employ of Prince Kamal Khan (Louis Jourdan). Accompanied by his saw, he goes on to threaten Bond and Octopussy (Maud Adams) in the Floating Palace.

TERENCE YOUNG: The original Bond director and helmsman of three of the four Bond films. Young was approached by Broccoli and Saltzman for *Dr No* after Guy Green and Bryan Forbes had turned the idea down. Young had worked with Broccoli in the past and was confident he could bring James Bond to life on the big screen.

He was also in the fortunate position of being one of the few directors to have worked with Sean Connery previously. Back in 1957, Young had directed the actor in *Action of the Tiger*. The two enjoyed a good working relationship and it was this that helped to create the screen image of Connery/Bond.

The best Bond film directed by Young is undoubtedly *From Russia With Love*. Its exotic style and mysterious characters perfectly suited Young's style. His last film, *Thunderball*, displays a slight uncertainty and disenchantment with the manner in which the series was evolving. Young's post-Bond work has included *Wait Until Dark* and *Bloodline*.

ZORA: A participant in the fight between the girls at the gypsy camp is Zora (Martine Beswick). Martine returns in *Thunderball* as Paula, 007's helper in Nassau.

MAX ZORIN: Leading French industrialist and staunch anti-communist, Max Zorin (Christopher Walken), the principal villain in *A View To A Kill*, has created a cover to fool secret services of the world. Zorin is a KGB agent but, during the course of the adventure, he becomes independent of his Soviet guardians. Born in Dresden, Zorin fled East Germany in the 1960s and became a French citizen. He speaks five languages with little accent. Money made from oil, gas, electronics and high-tech industries finances his wicked schemes.

Zorin's staff are loyal but bizarre. May Day (Grace Jones) is a muscle-bound black bodyguard who doubles as his lover. She is helped by Jenny Flex (Alison Doody) and Pan Ho (Papillon Soo Soo). Head of security is the scarred Scarpine (Patrick Bauchau).

Like most Bond villains he is rich. Zorin owns magnificent stables in France and is a keen horse breeder. He also owns an airship – G-BIHN – from which he conducts business meetings.

Zorin is mad, although he considers himself a genius. But this madness is tempered by hard-nosed business acumen. His scheme to destroy Silicon Valley is motivated by greed as he bids to corner the world's mircochip market.

His death is not confirmed by the film-makers and it seems possible Zorin may return to do battle with 007 once more.

ALSO AVAILABLE FROM
HODDER AND STOUGHTON PAPERBACKS